Rosie's

for Ty's *Beanie Babies*™

Editor and Collector: Rosie Wells

Published by Rosie Wells Enterprises, Inc.
22341 East Wells Rd., Canton, IL 61520
Phone: 1-309-668-2211   Fax: 1-309-668-2795
Check out our Web Site! http://www.RosieWells.com
E-mail address: RosieWells@aol.com
E-mail address to order publications:
Rosie@RosieWells.com

Table of Contents

A MESSAGE FROM THE EDITOR III

SHOW ME THE BEANIES! IV

UNDERSTANDING THE TAGS VI

HOW TO USE THIS GUIDE VIII

BEANIE BABIES 1

TEENIE BEANIE BABIES™/MC..122

RARE BEAR 124

BIRTHDAY ANNOUNCEMENTS 125

RETIREMENTS 127

OUT OF PRODUCTION 127

MY PERSONAL BEANIE BABIES™ COLLECTION© 133

Acknowledgements

Rosie Wells Enterprises, Inc., wishes to thank all who contributed in any way to help compile the information for this special premiere edition guide for Ty Inc. Beanie Babies™.

A special thanks to Peggy Gallagher and her husband, Daniel A. Gallagher, for photographs of their special Beanies Babies and information regarding the collection.

Thanks to Sara Nelson (www.BeanieMom.com) for information she has provided for us.

Thanks to Terry and Dusty Gohde and Lisa Harris for providing their Beanie Babies to photograph.

Thanks to the hard-working people in our art department; you make it all look so good!

A very special thanks to Rosie Wells; you inspire us with your knowledge of collectibles and special love for the collector. (Your Staff)

A special thanks to Ty, Inc. for such a great collectible. Keep up the good work!

From the Editor

Beanie Babies™ by Ty Inc., have taken the American scene by storm! They have become the favorite collectible of children, parents and grandparents. Truck drivers, teachers, doctors, lawyers… many have become enthralled by these delightful Beanie Babies toys. Collectors routinely line up outside small gift shops before opening time on the days when shipments of Beanie Babies have arrived the day before. Extra sales clerks are hired to keep up with the customers' rush to purchase, not to mention answering phone calls which come in one after another! Many retailers have set up message/answering machine services to accommodate the extra rings. Duplicate this same delirium all over the country and you have the most sensational collectible of the year: a line of small bean bag animals with names like *Quackers*™ the Duck and *Sly*™ the Fox, and quaint little poems written on Ty tags, the symbol of their authenticity.

Sold mainly in small gift shops, card shops, small toy stores and airport gift shops, Beanie Babies have often been hard to find. During the spring of 1997, Designer Ty Warner placed a limit on how many were sent to each store – no more than 36 of each character per month. Even then, most of the retailers received less than a third of that supply. Yet it seems the harder these Beanie Babies are to find, the more people want them! Add to that the Beanie Babies' retirements and the introductions twice a year, coupled with either mistakes or changes in production, you have the making of a most desirable collectible.

According to the best sources, the first nine of these plush, plastic pellet-filled animals were designed in 1992 and released in 1993. Since then, the Ty Company has introduced new Beanie Babies every six months. Those first released Beanie Babies included *Chocolate*™ the Moose, *Cubbie*™ the Bear, *Flash*™ the Dolphin, *Legs*™ the Frog, *Patti*™ the Platypus, *Spot*™ the Dog, *Splash*™ the Whale, *Squealer*™ the Pig and *Pinchers*™ the Lobster. All but *Flash*™ and *Splash*™ are still in production as of mid-1997. The wish for a complete collection, including retired Beanie Babies, has created a prospering secondary market.

Write to me and send photos of you and your Beanie Babies. I'd like to publish some to share with other collectors. You may wish to subscribe to the *Weekly Collectors' Gazette*™ to keep updated every week on what is happening with the Beanie Babies collection. For more collector news and photos, subscribe to the *Collectors' Bulletin*™! Just call my office for information on how to subscribe. Try my 1-900 hot line for Beanie Babies; call 1-900-740-7575 ($2 per minute using a touch tone phone, you must be 18 years old or older).

Enjoy this guide – I hope it adds to your pleasure of collecting Beanie Babies! I love 'em!

Rosie

Show Me The Beanies!

Patti

Beanie Babies have had changes made during production times. Most have been color changes but many included changes to materials used in production, pattern changes and name changes. The color change descriptions follow. *Bongo*™ the Monkey changed from the body and tail being the same color of brown to his tail being much lighter to match paws and face. *Digger*™ the Crab's color changed from orange to red. *Happy*™ the Hippo changed from the color gray to lavender. *Inky*™ the Octopus changed from being tan to pink. *Lizzy*™ the Lizard has undergone the change from having a tie-dyed fabric to having a blue and black fabric design with a yellow underbelly. *Magic*™ the Dragon changed from having its wing thread color being pale pink to hot pink. *Patti*™ the Platypus was one of the first Beanie Babies to have a color change. *Patti* was first produced with her fabric color being more of a magenta color. Now her color has a purple tint. *Peanut*™ the Elephant was first produced with a dark blue fabric that is now changed to a light blue fabric. *Spot*™ the Dog was first introduced without a black spot. *Sly*™ the Fox at first was produced with an all-brown body, white inner ears and muzzle, and then was changed to a brown body with a white belly, white inner ears and muzzle.

Changes to materials used in production include the following: *Inch*™ the Inchworm was first produced with felt antennas. Later the felt antennas were replaced with black yarn. *Derby*™ the Horse was first produced with a fine yarn mane and tail. Later productions find *Derby* with a coarser yarn for a mane and tail. *Mystic*™ the Unicorn also had a tail and mane change, only from coarse to soft fine yarn and back again to the coarser yarn.

Pattern Changes include: The Brown, Cranberry, Jade, Magenta, Teal and Violet *Teddy.*™ They were all produced in what is being known as an "old style" European bear face called a "*squirrel face*" and a "*round face,*" new style Teddy. *Quackers*™ the Duck was first produced, unbelievably, without wings.

Name Changes include: *Nana*™ the Monkey's name being changed to *Bongo*™ the Monkey. *Spooky*™ the Ghost was first known as Spook™.

Four Beanie Babies have gained the notable distinction of undergoing three definite changes. *Lucky*™ the Ladybug was first introduced with only seven, 9 mm in diameter, black felt spots which were glued onto her red back. This, of

Peanut

course, was not such a good idea for *Lucky,* as her spots would fall off! This initiated a change in *Lucky.* Her spots no longer numbered seven, nor were they glued on, but there were now eleven spots which were patterned into her fabric. Later, for reasons known only to the Ty Corp., *Lucky's* spots changed for a third time. *Lucky* is now being produced with approximately 21 smaller spots on her back.

Nip™ the Cat was first produced with a gold body and a white triangle on face and belly. This first *Nip* also had pink ears, nose and whiskers. The second *Nip* the Cat was produced a bit smaller and had an all gold body, pink ears and whiskers. The third *Nip* was produced with an all gold body with the exception of white paws, pink nose, white ears and whiskers.

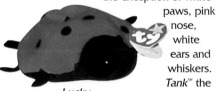

Lucky

Tank™ the Armadillo underwent three changes in production. First produced with seven stitched shell lines, the second version of *Tank* had nine stitched shell lines. Finally, the third version of *Tank* has the nine stitched shell lines and an extra line stitched along the bottom across the shell lines.

Zip™ the Cat was first produced with a black body and a white triangle on face and belly. This first *Zip* also had pink ears, nose and whiskers. The second *Zip* the Cat was produced a bit smaller and had an all black body, pink ears and whiskers. The third *Zip* was produced with an all black body, with exception of white paws, pink nose, white ears and whiskers.

McDonald's TBB

Knowing a good thing when they see it, McDonald's decided to offer ten miniature versions of Beanie Babies in their Happy Meals. Licensed by TY, Inc.,

but manufactured by McDonald's through their own sources, 100 million **Teenie Beanie Babies**™ were distributed to McDonald's restaurants. On April 11, 1997, McDonald's Teenie Beanie Babies were introduced. What was planned as a five week promotion, with two Teenie Beanie Babies given out

Chocolate in a bag

per week, lasted for considerably less time as the demand for these Teenie Beanie Babies was overwhelming. McDonald's did not even have the need to advertise the way they normally do for such promotions. In fact, a low key approach in advertising was used because McDonald's realized that they seriously underestimated the number of Teenie Beanie Babies it was going to need (particularly in the Midwest).

According to the October 21,1996, issue of *Forbes* magazine, "The strategy of the Beanie Babies craze is empty shelves – the deliberate creation of scarcity, which pumps up word-of-mouth demand to a frenzied level." This has been the practice of marketing the Beanie Babies™ which also seems to be working to create an exciting secondary market.

Much of the information for this review was obtained from our Beanie archives of literature including Peggy Gallagher's articles from our *Collectors' Bulletin*™ and from Peggy's Vol. I booklet *The Beanie Baby Phenomenon! (see ad on page 130).*

The Swing Tag

There are four generation Ty swing tags. The first, second and third generation tags are now retired. The first generation Ty swing tag is a single tag. On the back it reads:

> **The Beanie Babies Collection**
> Beanies' name, style number
> ©1993 Ty Inc. Oakbrook, IL, USA
> All Rights Reserved Caution
> Remove this tag before giving
> toy to a child. For ages 5 and up
> Handmade in China
> Surface
> Wash

The second generation Ty swing tag is a double tag. On the inside of this tag, which opens like a book, it reads:

> **The Beanie Babies Collection**
> Beanies' name, style number
> ©1993 Ty Inc. Oakbrook, IL, USA
> All Rights Reserved Caution
> Remove this tag before giving
> toy to a child. For ages 5 and up
> Handmade in China
> Surface
> Wash

> The Beanies' name and Style number
> to _____
> from _____
> with
> love

The third generation Ty swing tag is also a double tag. The Ty lettering is in a much larger font type. On the inside of this tag it reads:

> **The Beanie Babies Collection**
> © Ty Inc
> Oakbrook, IL. USA
>
> Ty UK Ltd.
> Waterlooville, Hants
> PO8 8HH
>
> Ty Deutschland
> 90008 Nurnberg
>
> Handmade in China

> The Beanies' name and Style number
> to _____
> from_____
> with
> love

The fourth generation Ty swing tag is also a double tag. During the summer of '96 a white sticker was placed on the tag covering the Ty web site address. This was done because the Web site was not fully operational. Do not remove this sticker as this actually dates these Beanie Babies as being produced for the summer of '96. On the inside of this tag it reads:

> **The Beanie Babies Collection**
> © Ty Inc
> Oakbrook, IL. USA
>
> Ty UK Ltd.
> Waterlooville, Hants
> PO8 8HH
>
> Ty Deutschland
> 90008 Nurnberg
>
> Handmade in China

> The Beanies' name and Style number
> Date of Birth
> Poem
>
> Visit our web page!!!
> http://www.ty.com

Errored Tags

Beanie Babies come with a heart-shaped paper TY swing tag and a fabric sewn-in tush tag. Errors to these tags have been recorded in this guide. At this time it is felt that errors to TY swing tags may not be that significant to the secondary market value of the piece. The swing tags are easily changed, and to pay more for Beanie Babies with the wrong swing tag may not be advisable. The errored tush tag, however, may be more significant due to the fact that it would be difficult to purposely change a tush tag.

The Tush Tag

```
© 1993 TY INC.,
OAKBROOK IL. U.S.A.
ALL RIGHTS RESERVED
HAND MADE IN CHINA
SURFACE WASHABLE
```

```
ALL NEW MATERIAL
POLYESTER FIBER
PA. REG #1965
FOR AGES 3 AND UP
```

In most cases, the type of tush tag that your Beanie Baby has suggests the approximate age of your Beanie Baby. Beanie Babies produced in 1994 have the 1993 tush tag.

The first generation tush tag (left) had black ink printed on white fabric. This was produced in 1993 and the same design was used for the 1995 black inked tush tag.

The second generation tush tag (right) had red ink on white fabric. (Both the second and third generation tush tag can also be found with the words "Made in Korea.") It has 1993 or 1995 printed on it and does not have the name of the Beanie Baby on it.

```
HAND MADE IN CHINA
© 1993 TY INC.,
OAKBROOK IL. U.S.A.
SURFACE WASHABLE
ALL NEW MATERIAL
POLYESTER FIBER &
P.V.C. PELLETS
REG. NO PA1965(KR)
                    CE
```

```
The
Beanie Babies
Collection™

ty ®

Spooky
```

The third generation tush tags (left) also had red ink on white fabric and included the name of the Beanie Baby. It has 1993, 1995 or 1996 printed on it.

```
HAND MADE IN CHINA
© 1993 TY INC.,
OAKBROOK IL. U.S.A.
SURFACE WASHABLE
ALL NEW MATERIAL
POLYESTER FIBER
& P.V.C. PELLETS   CE
REG. NO PA 1965(KR)
```

There are two tags found on all Beanie Babies produced for Canada. Along with the third generation tush tag, the Canadian tush tag (see page 59) is larger and uses black ink on white fabric. It must be attached to all Beanie Babies that are made for distribution in Canada.

Also, an embroidered cloth tush tag (not shown) has been found on some Beanie Babies. It is thought that this tag is used for other Ty products in the plush line and that it has inadvertently been placed on some of the Beanie Babies, mainly those which were made for Canadian distribution.

More recently, a new tush tag (right) has been seen on all currently produced Beanie Babies. In mid-1997, the red and white tush tag (with the name) adds a star to the left of the Ty heart. Temporarily, this is accomplished by a clear sticker with only a star printed on it being placed over the Ty heart so that the star is to the left of the heart. We assume this will be replaced by a permanent tag. Do not remove these stickers as they date the Beanie Babies as mid-1997 productions!

```
The
Beanie Babies
Collection™

★ ty ®

Ziggy
```

How to Use this Guide

Beanie Babies™ are listed Alphabetically in this guide.
A Subject Reference for Beanie Babies can be found on page 129.
Secondary market values are for Beanie Babies with tags that are in mint
condition. For more information on tags see page VI.

 *Look for our symbol to readily signify the elite
"First 9 Beanie Babies™ " produced.*

① Beanie Babies photos which include all Versions with, in this example, the
most current Version being number 3. Most Beanie Babies produced by Ty, Inc.,
come in only one Version and thus only one picture will be found on the page.

② Poem which would be found on the fourth generation swing tag. Not all
Beanie Babies came with the fourth generation swing tag and hence did not have
a poem. All poems are the property of Ty Corporation.

③ Style number and name of Beanie Baby.

④ Instant Alert - Do I, or do I not have this piece? If this piece is a part of your
collection, place a check √ in the box. In this example there are three Versions of
Lucky which are possible to own. Mark the Version you have, either
☐1 ☐2 ☐3 or maybe all three!!

⑤ Comments: Contains year of issue, birthdate and issue price. Also included within
these comments will be descriptions of all Versions and secondary market values for
the earliest Versions of the Beanie Baby.

⑥ During the Spring and Summer of '97 (**S/S**), original retail for Beanie Babies aver-
aged between $5-$6, but $7.50-$20 was common at some retail outlets. While vaca-
tioning in St. Louis, during the Summer of '97, I found that it was not unusual to see
Beanie Babies retailing for $8-$10. One chain store, which has over 100 stores, was
selling current Beanie Babies for $7.50 each and they were selling out! The scarcity of
'97 S/S brought on this frenzy. Current Beanie Babies have been sold by internet
entrepreneurs, individuals at secondary market shows and collectors selling Beanie
Babies through classified ads. These folks were able to easily sell current Beanie Babies
for $10 to $20. Beanie Babies' production will hopefully return to "how it was" before
the scarce Spring and Summer of '97. Then, perhaps, current Beanie Babies may be
back to the initial retail prices of $5-$6... Time will tell. This guide gives **S/S** prices,
which represent the averages for the **'97 "Spring/Summer"** Secondary Market Values.
No other guide offers this research of **'97 Spring/Summer Secondary Market Values**
for you to use when reselling or insuring your current Beanie Babies.™

⑦ For your personal record keeping.

Lucky™ the Ladybug

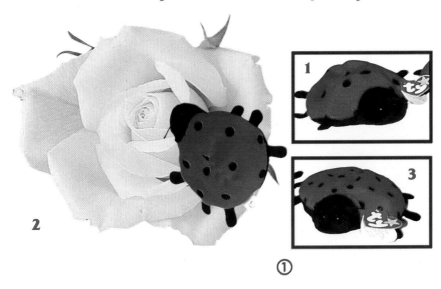

② Lucky the ladybug loves the lotto
"Someone must win" that's her motto
But save your dimes and even a penny
Don't spend on the lotto and you'll have many!

③ **4040**   **Lucky the Ladybug**   1 2 3 ④

⑤ *COMMENTS:* Issued 1994, Birthday 5/1/95, Issue Price $5 - $6
Like most ladies, this ladybug cannot make up her mind over what she
wants to wear. In Version 1, she first wore a coat of seven, 9mm, black
felt spots glued onto her red back and a second generation Ty tag. The
secondary market value of Version 1 is $85-$100. In Version 2, a
change to eleven black spots, which were part of the fabric was what
this fine lady wore. Finally, Version 3 of Lucky comes with 21 small,
6mm spots as part of the fabric. She also has been found with a Bucky
tush tag; she just laughed about that.

⑥ **Secondary Market Value: S/S $10-$12 (Versions 2 & 3)**

⑦ Purchase Date_____ From_____ Price Paid $ _____

_____

_____

Kids + Beanie Babies™ That's what it's all about!

Clockwise from top left

1. Strollin' with Beanies
2. Hannah wins look-a-like contest!
3. Young entrepreneurs on the Beanie Trail
4. Just can't get enough Beanies!
5. Hunter, Rosie's grandson, swingin' with his Beanies

Ally™ the Alligator

When Ally gets out of classes
He wears a hat and dark glasses
He plays bass in a street band
He's the coolest gator in the land!

4032   **Ally the Alligator**   ☐
               CURRENT
COMMENTS: Issued 1994, Birthday 3/14/94, Issue Price $5-$6
Ally is really cool, just don't be caught with him in the pool.
Ally has been found with Patti's tag. Patti was pretty upset about
it, but they've made up. Quite scarce mid-1997!
Secondary Market Value: S/S $18-$22
Purchase Date_____ From_____ Price Paid $ _____

_____

_____

Baldy™ the Eagle

Hair on his head is quite scant
We suggest Baldy get a transplant
Watching over the land of the free
Hair in his eyes would make it hard to see!

4074   **Baldy the Eagle**   ☐
CURRENT

COMMENTS: Issued 1997, Birthday 2/17/96, Issue Price $5-$6
Baldy soars and glides high in the air, you'll find it hard not to stare.
Baldy debuted in Spring of '97 but was very scarce due to the fact
that only 36 per style could be ordered by retailers. Eagle collectors searched high and low for him when he debuted.

Secondary Market Value: S/S $20-$22

Purchase Date_____ From_____ Price Paid $ _____

Bernie™ the Saint Bernard

This little dog can't wait to grow
To rescue people lost in the snow
Don't let him out - keep him on your shelf
He doesn't know how to rescue himself!

4109   **Bernie the Saint Bernard**   ☐
               CURRENT
COMMENTS: Issued 1997, Birthday 10/3/96, Issue Price $5-$6
What a cute puppy for you to hold, and a great friend, or so I'm told.
This puppy was popular and abundant when he debuted. Cute!
Secondary Market Value: S/S $12-$15
Purchase Date_____ From_____ Price Paid $ _____

_____

_____

Bessie™ the Cow

Bessie the cow likes to dance and sing
Because music is her favorite thing
Every night when you're counting sheep
She'll sing you a song to put you sleep!

4009   **Bessie the Cow**   ☐
                      CURRENT
COMMENTS: Issued 1995, Birthday 6/27/95, Issue Price $5-$6
Cow collectors love Bessie… Expect to pay up to $40 for the older
black and white tush tag.
Secondary Market Value: S/S $10-$15
Purchase Date_____ From_____ Price Paid $ _____

_____

_____

Blackie™ the Bear

Living in a national park
He only played after dark
Then he met his friend Cubbie
Now they play when it's sunny!

4011   **Blackie the Bear**   ☐
            CURRENT

COMMENTS: Issued 1994, Birthday 7/15/94, Issue Price $5-$6
Blackie was produced to lay on his tummy. He is still available at
press time with a current fourth generation Ty tag. He is very hard
to find with the third generation Ty tag, and you can expect to pay
up to $40 for that tag. Blackie has been found with three factory
attached eyes! Very odd, indeed! Better to find honey! He is a
good retirement candidate.
Secondary Market Value: S/S $10-$12
Purchase Date_____ From_____ Price Paid $ _____

Blizzard™ the White Tiger

In the mountains, where it's snowy and cold
Lives a beautiful tiger, I've been told
Black and white, she's hard to compare
Of all the tigers, she is most rare!

4163   Blizzard the White Tiger

CURRENT
COMMENTS: Issued 1997, Birthday 12/12/96, Issue Price $5-$6
Blizzard is a popular Tiger! Will be around for awhile!
Secondary Market Value: S/S $18-$25
Purchase Date_____ From_____ Price Paid $ _____

_____

_____

Bones™ the Dog

Bones is a dog that loves to chew
Chairs and tables and a smelly old shoe
"You're so destructive" all would shout
But that all stopped, when his teeth fell out!

4001   **Bones the Dog**   ☐

CURRENT

COMMENTS: Issued 1995, Birthday 1/18/94, Issue Price $5-$6
Bones's tag has been found with the word "Your" instead of
"You're" in the third line of his poem. He really doesn't seem to
care, because he knows everyone who collects Beanies just has to
have him! A popular selling "Pillow Pal" by the Ty Co., is Woof.™
You need one! Place li'l Bones, maybe three or four of these guys,
next to Woof. What a great family! ARF!

Secondary Market Value: S/S $20-$25

Purchase Date_____ From_____ Price Paid $ _____

_____

_____

Bongo™ the Monkey

2

1

Bongo the monkey lives in a tree
He's the happiest monkey you'll ever see
In his spare time he plays the guitar
One of these days he will be a big star!

4067   **Bongo the Monkey**   1 2
              CURRENT

COMMENTS: Issued 1995, Birthday 8/17/95, Issue Price $5-$6
Bongo was first produced with his tail the same color as his body. He also had a third generation swing tag and second generation tush tag without the name (Version 1). Many of these first Bongos were found with a sticker over the name on the swing tag. This covered up the name Nana. Do not remove the sticker, as this helps to identify the approximate time of production. Version 1 would have a secondary market value of $150-$165. In early '96, Bongo's tail was produced with the lighter material which matches his face (Version 2). Soon after, the color of Bongo's tail reverted back to the same color as his body. Watch the swing and tush tags when placing a value on this Beanie Baby.
Secondary Market Value: S/S $12-$15
Purchase Date_____ From_____ Price Paid $ _____

Bronty™ the Brontosaurus

4085   **Bronty the Brontosaurus**   ☐

RETIRED 4/96

COMMENTS: Issued 1995, Issue Price $5-$6

Bronty debuted with the third generation Ty tag. Handle him with care because his seams have been known to open and he has lost his little pellets. Bronty is the most scarce of the three dinosaurs.

Secondary Market Value: $400-$475

Purchase Date_____ From_____ Price Paid $ _____

Brownie™ the Bear

4010   **Brownie the Bear**   ☐

OUT OF PRODUCTION

COMMENTS: Issued 1993, Birthday 11/14/93, Issue Price $5-$6
Brownie was one of the original nine Ty Beanie Babies to be intro-
duced in 1994. His name was soon changed to Cubbie. See
Cubbie on page 23.

Secondary Market Value: $600-$650

Purchase Date_____ From_____ Price Paid $ _____

_____

_____

Bubbles™ the Fish

All day long Bubbles likes to swim
She never gets tired of flapping her fins
Bubbles lived in a sea of blue
Now she is ready to come home with you!

4078   **Bubbles the Fish**   ☐

RETIRED 5/11/97

COMMENTS: Issued 1995, Birthday 7/2/95, Issue Price $5-$6
Bubbles has been found with two right sides sewn together, and so one fin is higher than the other. Perhaps she swims in circles? She has also been found with a blank Ty tag. Bubbles debuted with the second generation Ty tag, as well as with the third and fourth generation Ty tag. Remember, Ty swing tags can be easily changed using a special tagging gun which retailers use to tag merchandise.

Secondary Market Value: $50-$55

Purchase Date_____ From_____ Price Paid $ _____

Bucky™ the Beaver

His teeth are shiny as can be
Often used for cutting trees
He hides in his dam night and day
Maybe for you he will come out and play!

4016   **Bucky the Beaver**   ☐
          CURRENT
COMMENTS: Issued 1995, Birthday 6/8/95, Issue Price $5-$6
A favorite for the boys! May be a candidate for retirement in the future.
Secondary Market Value: S/S $11-$15
Purchase Date_____ From_____ Price Paid $ _____

_____

_____

Bumble™ the Bee

Bumble the bee will not sting you
It is only love that this bee will bring you
So don't be afraid to give this bee a hug
Because Bumble the bee is a love-bug!

4045   **Bumble the Bee**   ☐

RETIRED 4/96

COMMENTS: Issued 1995, Issue Price $5-$6
Before retirement, Bumble was produced with the third generation
Ty tag. After his retirement there were some lucky accounts that
received Bumble with the fourth generation poem tag. Bumble
with a fourth generation tag is very scarce.
Secondary Market Value: 3rd tag ~$175, 4th tag ~$225
Purchase Date_____ From_____ Price Paid $ _____

_____

_____

Caw™ the Crow

4071   Caw the Crow   ☐
RETIRED 4/96
COMMENTS: Issued 1995, Issue Price $5-$6
Caw was introduced in mid-1995 with the Ty third generation tag
which had the words "to," "from" and "with love" as well as the
Beanie name and style number. Very popular! Find him if you can!
Secondary Market Value: $200-$220
Purchase Date_____ From_____ Price Paid $ _____
_____
_____

Chilly the Polar Bear

4012   Chilly the Polar Bear

RETIRED 4/96

COMMENTS: Issued 1995, Issue Price $5-$6

Chilly was produced to lay on his tummy and had the third generation Ty tag which did not include a poem. Though a very coveted
bear, he debuted and layed on shelves before collectors knew
about Beanie Babies' future!

Secondary Market Value: $775-$825

Purchase Date_____ From_____ Price Paid $ _____

_____

_____

Chip™ the Cat

Black and gold, brown and white
The shades of her coat are quite a sight
At mixing her colors she was a master
On anyone else it would be a disaster!

4121   **Chip the Cat**   ☐
              CURRENT

COMMENTS: Issued 1997, Birthday 1/26/96, Issue Price $5-$6
Issued in 1997, Chip the Cat is a hit with cat lovers! There never
has been a "male" calico cat, from what I've heard! Eventually,
we're going to see some "retired" cats, in my opinion.
Display your kittens in a basket with balls of yarn.
Secondary Market Value: S/S $15-20
Purchase Date_____ From_____ Price Paid $ _____

Chocolate™ the Moose

Licorice, gum and peppermint candy
This moose always has these handy
There is one more thing he likes to eat
Can you guess his favorite sweet?

4015　　　　**Chocolate the Moose**　　　　☐
　　　　CURRENT

COMMENTS: Issued 1993, Birthday 4/27/93, Issue Price $5-$6
Chocolate was one of the first nine released in 1993, and is still being produced today with the current Ty poem tag. His first tag was the second generation Ty tag which did not include a poem. This older, mint condition, tagged Chocolate may bring up to $40 on the secondary market. He is very, very popular. Should he be retired in the future, he will be sought after! A great gift for men an boys! Chocolate the Moose was offered by McDonald's as a Teenie Beanie for an April '97 promotion. He was hot!
Secondary Market Value: S/S $12-15
Purchase Date_____ From_____ Price Paid $ _____

Chops™ the Lamb

Chops is a little lamb
This lamb you'll surely know
Because every path that you may take
This lamb is sure to go!

4019   **Chops the Lamb**   ☐
RETIRED 1/1/97

COMMENTS: Issued 1996, Birthday 5/3/96, Issue Price $5-$6
Chops has been found with his poem reading "surly know" instead
of the correct "surely know." Add only $5 to the secondary market
value for this error, as it's plentiful! Chops has been found with an
upside down ear and with one of his hind legs shorter than the
other. As a farm hand, I'd say a pack of wild dogs hit his flock!
Chops has been found without a mouth. When retired, Chops was
somewhat scarce and became more plentiful as retailers received it
after the retirement date. Fleece debuted in January '97, thus satis-
fying some folks' desire to own a lamb. Chops the Lamb was
offered as a Teenie Beanie by McDonald's for an April '97 promotion.
Secondary Market Value: $75-$95
Purchase Date_____ From_____ Price Paid $ _____

Claude™ the Crab

Claude the crab paints by the sea
A famous artist he hopes to be
But the tide came in and his paints fell
Now his art is on his shell!

4083　　　　**Claude the Crab**　　　　☐
　　　　　　CURRENT
COMMENTS: Issued 1997, Birthday 9/3/96, Issue Price $5-$6
Claude debuted just after Digger the Crab retired! Digger's red
color brightened one's collection but was not a favorite unless you
lived in the northeastern states! Sorry, Digger, but Claude will be a
faster seller due to the popular tie-dyed material!
Secondary Market Value: S/S $15-$20
Purchase Date_____ From_____ Price Paid $ _____

Congo™ the Gorilla

Black as the night and fierce is he
On the ground or in a tree
Strong and mighty as the Congo
He's related to our Bongo!

4106   **Congo the Gorilla**   ☐
              CURRENT
COMMENTS: Issued 1996, Birthday 11/9/96, Issue Price $5-$6
Congo has been found with a sewn-in tag that reads "Sly." Isn't
Congo the greatest?! I have seen a Tarzan suit designed for him!
Ha! He's a must have, and be sure you have Bongo to accompany
him, as they are buddies! Display them in a dish of plastic bananas!
Secondary Market Value: S/S $11-$14
Purchase Date_____ From_____ Price Paid $ _____

_____

_____

$\mathcal{C}oral^{™}$ the $\mathcal{F}ish$

Coral is beautiful, as you know
Made of colors in the rainbow
Whether it's pink, yellow or blue
These colors were chosen just for you!

4079   **Coral the Fish**   ☐
RETIRED 1/1/97

COMMENTS: Issued 1995, Birthday 3/2/95, Issue Price $5-$6
Coral was found with a Peanut sewn-in tag in late '96. Another
oddity was Coral with one eye larger than the other. Bubbles, the
other fish, retired in May of '97. Goldie remains. Be sure to get
her!! Display her in a fish bowl with large blue plastic pebbles! Add
some greenery! Nice!

Secondary Market Value: $65-$85

Purchase Date_____ From_____ Price Paid $ _____

_____

_____

Crunch™ the Shark

What's for breakfast? What's for lunch?
Yum! Delicious! Munch, munch, munch!
He's eating everything by the bunch
That's the reason we named him Crunch!

4130   Crunch the Shark   ☐

CURRENT

COMMENTS: Issued 1997, Birthday 1/13/96, Issue Price $5-$6
Poor Crunch! Everyone hopes he's the next to get retired. Li'l boys
like Crunch anyway!

Secondary Market Value: S/S $6-$10

Purchase Date_____ From_____ Price Paid $ _____

_____

_____

Cubbie™ the Bear

Cubbie used to eat crackers and honey
And what happened to him was funny
He was stung by fourteen bees
Now Cubbie eats broccoli and cheese!

4010   **Cubbie the Bear**   ☐
        CURRENT
COMMENTS: Issued 1993, Birthday 11/14/93, Issue Price $5-$6
This bear was produced to lay on his tummy and was first named
Brownie. He is now found with the current poem Ty tag. The
Chicago Cubs gave him away during a kids promotion on May 18,
'97. Shall we see a "Cardinal" Beanie Baby soon?
Secondary Market Value: S/S $10-$12
Purchase Date_____ From_____ Price Paid $ _____

Curly™ the Bear

A bear so cute with hair that's curly
You will love and want him surely
To this bear always be true
He will be a friend to you!

4052   **Curly the Bear**   ☐

CURRENT

COMMENTS: Issued 1996, Birthday 4/12/96, Issue Price $5-$6
Curly has nappy fabric instead of the usual plush texture fabric.
Curly was produced to sit up and has only been seen with the
current Ty poem tag. He may debut in a different color or his pal,
Teddy, may debut in a different color. Both are good retirement
candidates.

Secondary Market Value: S/S $12-$15

Purchase Date_____ From_____ Price Paid $ _____

Daisy™ the Cow

Daisy drinks milk each night
So her coat is shiny and bright
Milk is good for your hair and skin
What a way for your day to begin!

4006   **Daisy the Cow**   ☐
              CURRENT
COMMENTS: Issued 1994, Birthday 5/10/94, Issue Price $5-$6
Cow collectors look for Daisy... She's hoping "Casey" the bull will
debut soon. She's not interested in a "red" bull! Wrong breed, she
said! She wants a Holstein guy!
Secondary Market Value: S/S $10-$12
Purchase Date_____ From_____ Price Paid $ _____

_____

_____

Derby™ the Horse

All the other horses used to tattle
Because Derby never wore his saddle
He left the stables, and the horses too
Just so Derby can be with you!

4008   **Derby the Horse**   1 2
CURRENT

COMMENTS: Issued 1995, Birthday 9/16/95, Issue Price $5-$6
Derby the Horse came first with his tail and mane made from fine
yarn (Version 1). Prices being paid for a fine mane Derby range
from $450-$500, with possible expectations to exceed even $800
to $950 by mid-1998, say several experts on Beanie Babies. Since
'96, a coarser yarn has been used for his mane and tail (Version 2).
Popular and scarce even before the "dry period" of Spring, 1997!
Secondary Market Value: S/S $15-$18

Purchase Date_____ From_____ Price Paid $ _____

Digger™ the Crab

Digging in the sand and walking sideways
That's how Digger spends her days
Hard on the outside but sweet deep inside
Basking in the sun, riding the tide!

4027   **Digger the Crab**   1   2

RETIRED 5/11/97

COMMENTS: Issued 1995, Birthday 8/23/95, Issue Price $5-$6
Digger first appeared as an orange crab with the first generation Ty
tag. This version is very scarce (Version 1). The orange Digger's
secondary market price is $325-$375. Red Digger replaced the
orange Digger in late 1995 (Version 2). Since the red Digger
retired in May of '97, very few shipments were received through
June. If no further shipments of Digger are received and this
becomes a "drop dead retirement," expect prices to zoom up to
$85 in late '97.

Secondary Market Value: $45-$55

Purchase Date_____ From_____ Price Paid $ _____

Doby™ the Doberman

This dog is little but he has might
Keep him close when you sleep at night
He lays around with nothing to do
Until he sees its time to protect you!

4110   **Doby the Doberman**   ☐
                CURRENT
COMMENTS: Issued 1997, Birthday 10/9/96, Issue Price $5-$6
Many thought ole Doby looked more like a rottweiler. One has to
remember, he's just a pup without his ears trimmed! OUCH!
Secondary Market Value: S/S $8-$10
Purchase Date_____ From_____ Price Paid $ _____

_____

_____

Doodle™ the Rooster

Listen closely to "Cock-a-doodle-doo"
What's the rooster saying to you?
Hurry, wake up sleepy head
We have lots to do, get out of bed!

4171   **Doodle the Rooster**   ☐

                  CURRENT

COMMENTS: Issued 1997, Birthday 3/8/96, Issue Price $5-$6
A favorite for many! He's so colorful! Let's hope next year we will
see his "Sweet Chick!" Very scarce during its spring and summer
debut!

Secondary Market Value: S/S $18-$25

Purchase Date_____ From_____ Price Paid $ _____

_____

_____

Dotty™ the Dalmatian

The Beanies all thought it was a big joke
While writing her tag, their ink pen broke
She got in the way, and got all spotty,
So now the Beanies call her Dotty!

4100   **Dotty the Dalmatian**   ☐
            CURRENT
COMMENTS: Issued 1997, Birthday 10/17/96, Issue Price $5-$6
Sparky the Dalmatian retired, but mid-1997 Sparky came out with
a "Dotty" tag. This Sparky with Dotty tag reached the $40 mark
soon after... It's my opinion, "Buyer Beware." Tags from Dotty
could easily be switched to Sparky with the Sparky tush tag.
Secondary Market Value: S/S $12-$15
Purchase Date_____ From_____ Price Paid $ _____

Ears™ the Bunny

He's been eating carrots so long
Didn't understand what was wrong
Couldn't see the board during classes
Until the doctor gave him glasses!

4018   **Ears the Bunny**   □
            CURRENT
COMMENTS: Issued 1996, Birthday 4/18/95, Issue Price $5-$6
Ears the Bunny was found in certain carrot patches with either
Manny or Scoop swing tags. Ears became scarce about the time
the Easter Bunny came last spring... during that time he brought
S/S prices! I have my Ears in a carrot designed sleeping bag! Ears
might be a good retirement candidate!
Secondary Market Value: S/S $12-$18
Purchase Date_____ From_____ Price Paid $ _____
_____
_____

Echo™ the Dolphin

Echo the dolphin lives in the sea
Playing with her friends like you and me
Through the waves she echoes the sound
"I'm so glad to have you around!"

4084   **Echo the Dolphin**   ☐

CURRENT

COMMENTS: Issued 1997, Birthday 12/21/96, Issue Price $5-$6
Don't get excited... all Echos first debuted with "Waves" the Orca
Whale's tag, and Waves had "Echo's" tag... Do not over-pay to
own either of these two for that reason for at least a year!
Secondary Market Value: S/S $15-$20
Purchase Date_____ From_____ Price Paid $ _____

Flash™ the Dolphin

You know dolphins are the smartest breed
Well Flash the dolphin knows how to read
She's teaching her friend Splash to read too
So maybe one day they can both read to you.

4021   **Flash the Dolphin**   ☐
                 RETIRED 5/11/97
COMMENTS: Issued 1993, Birthday 5/13/93, Issue Price $5-$6
One of the original nine Beanie Babies, Flash has the first genera-
tion Ty tag. She could have an old Ty tag that says "Fiash." Flash
was also found with Bones, Chocolate, Daisy, Mystic and Patti tags!
Flash was somewhat of a slow seller. Probably why he retired.
Secondary Market Value: $35-$50
Purchase Date_____ From_____ Price Paid $ _____

_____

_____

33

Fleece™ the Lamb

Fleece would like to sing a lullaby
But please be patient, she's rather shy
When you sleep, keep her by your ear
Her song will leave you nothing to fear!

4125   **Fleece the Lamb**   ☐
              CURRENT

COMMENTS: Issued 1997, Birthday 3/21/96, Issue Price $5-$6
"You can count on this lamb to be a favorite!" Fleece has a soft
nappy fabric, instead of plush, and a fourth generation Ty tag with
the red ink body tag. Bernie, Lizzy and Nuts tush tags have been
found on Fleece. Fleece was somewhat scarce when she debuted
and through the '97 spring and early summer. She started to
return to the shelves in mid-June of '97. Nice one!

Secondary Market Value: S/S $15-$20

Purchase Date_____ From_____ Price Paid $ _____

_____

_____

Flip™ the Cat

Flip the cat is an acrobat
She loves playing on her mat
This cat flips with such grace and flair
She can somersault in mid-air!

4012   **Flip the Cat**   ☐
                CURRENT
COMMENTS: Issued 1996, Birthday 2/28/95, Issue Price $5-$6
This white cat with pink whiskers, nose and inner ears has been
found with a Kiwi or a Wrinkles tush tag. Flip has been more scarce
than the other cats. Eventually, we're going to see some cats
retired! Flip is really popular and somewhat scarce, even during
the abundant times.
Secondary Market Value: S/S $15-$20
Purchase Date_____ From_____ Price Paid $ _____
_____
_____

Floppity™ the Rabbit

Floppity hops from here to there
Searching for eggs without a care
Lavender coat from head to toe
All dressed up and nowhere to go!

4118   **Floppity the Rabbit**   ☐
              CURRENT
COMMENTS: Issued 1997, Birthday 5/28/96, Issue Price $5-$6
A Lucky tush tag has also been found on this rabbit. Hopefully,
we'll see more of these rabbits by next Easter! Everyone thinks
these "three" pastel bunnies are on their way to retirement. I think
all, or at least two, will be around for Easter '98. How about a light
blue rabbit next? Have heard a "Prototype" of Floppity was found
in England with a tag (not Ty) which had the phrase "QC Sample"
handwritten on it.
Secondary Market Value: S/S $20-$25
Purchase Date_____ From_____ Price Paid $ _____

4043   **Flutter the Butterfly**   ☐
           RETIRED 4/96
COMMENTS: Issued 1995, Issue Price $5-$6
Many collectors would enjoy finding this one on a dealer's shelf,
but there's not a very good chance of that. Flutter was for sale at
retail before most of us knew what Beanie Babies were! What is it
they say about hindsight?
Secondary Market Value: $375-$450
Purchase Date_____ From_____ Price Paid $ _____

_____

_____

Freckles™ the Leopard

From the trees he hunts his prey
In the night and in the day
He's the king of camouflage
Look real close he's no mirage!

4066   **Freckles the Leopard**   ① ②

CURRENT

COMMENTS: Issued 1996, Birthday 6/03/96, Issue Price $5-$6
Freckles has also been found with the birth date 7/28/96 on his tag.
White stitching around his nose has been reported. He was also produced with a thicker, more plush fabric as in Version 1. Tush tag errors
include a Squealer tush tag and no tag at all. Curiously enough, Freckles
has been found with production errors. He has been found missing a
leg… another with a missing nose, another missing eyes and another
missing whiskers. Ah, poor Freckles! Missing body parts would be high
on the secondary market if the missing part has not been removed after
it left the retailer's shelf! How else could anyone know unless it is found
by yourself at the retailers? Collectors take extra caution when buying
on secondary market on missing parts. Freckles is very popular!
Secondary Market Value: S/S $12-$15

Purchase Date_____ From_____ Price Paid $ _____

Garcia™ the Bear

The Beanies use to follow him around
Because Garcia traveled from town to town
He's pretty popular as you can see
Some even say he's legendary

4051   **Garcia the Bear**   ☐

RETIRED 5/11/97

COMMENTS: Issued 1995, Birthday 8/1/95, Issue Price $5-$6
Garcia has been designed to sit up. "No two alike" could be said of
Garcia. Very popular as he is rumored to have been named after
the singer, Jerry Garcia. A poem error such as "The Beanies used to
follow him around" instead of "use to" pops up. Garcias from
Canada have two tush tags, and many during the winter of '96,
were found to be more colorful than those found in the States at
that time. Prices even before retirement were $25-$30 and rose to
$75 just after retirement. More came from Ty company to dealers
in May '97. Prices fell to $35-$40 by late June. Prices may go up if
Ty Co., doesn't ship more after S/S. I look for more. **PROBABLY
THE "MOST POPULAR" BEANIE BABY TO DATE!**
Secondary Market Value: $40-$55
Purchase Date_____ From_____ Price Paid $ _____

Goldie™ the Goldfish

She's got the rhythm, she's got the soul
What more could you want in a fish bowl?
Through sound waves Goldie swam
Because this goldfish likes to jam.

4023   **Goldie the Goldfish**   ☐
              CURRENT
COMMENTS: Issued 1994, Birthday 11/14/94, Issue Price $5-$6
Look out, fish world! This dashing fish swims with ALL FOUR Ty
generation tags. For her oldest tag, the secondary market prices
have been seen from $30-$40. She has been found swimming
around with a Lizzy tush tag. Will Goldie be retired soon? Her two
pals, Coral and Bubbles, were retired. Goldie was also a
McDonald's Teenie Beanie!
Secondary Market Value: S/S $10-$15
Purchase Date_____ From_____ Price Paid $ _____

Gracie™ the Swan

As a duckling, she was confused
Birds on the lake were quite amused
Poking fun until she would cry,
Now the most beautiful swan at Ty!

4126   **Gracie the Swan**   ☐
                  CURRENT

COMMENTS: Issued 1997, Birthday 6/17/96, Issue Price $5-$6
Gracie the "ugly duckling" also has been found with a Bones swing
tag and a Bucky tush tag. Gracie and Crunch debuted together
and, sorry to say, they were the last to leave the shelves. Sorry,
Gracie... They may be good candidates for retirement! Place a
straw hat on Gracie. It perks her up!
Secondary Market Value: S/S $6-$10
Purchase Date_____ From_____ Price Paid $ _____

Grunt™ the Razorback

Some Beanies think Grunt is tough
No surprise, he's scary enough
But if you take him home you'll see
Grunt is the sweetest Beanie Baby!

4092   **Grunt the Razorback**   ☐
                   RETIRED 5/11/97
COMMENTS: Issued 1995, Birthday 7/19/95, Issue Price $5-$6
Poor ole Grunt - just didn't sell well... many didn't have him when
he retired. Red Beanie Babies brighten up displays.
Secondary Market Value: S/S $45-$60
Purchase Date_____ From_____ Price Paid $ _____

_____

_____

Happy™ the Hippo

Happy the Hippo loves to wade
In the river and in the shade
When Happy shoots water out of his snout
You know he's happy without a doubt!

4061   **Happy the Hippo**   ① ②
         CURRENT
COMMENTS: Issued 1994, Birthday 2/25/94, Issue Price $5-$6
Introduced in '94, shortly after the original nine, Happy was first
produced as a light gray hippo with a second generation Ty tag
(Version 1). Happy's fabric was then changed to lavender and
released with a third generation Ty tag and red ink body tag
(Version 2). Version 1's price ranges from $275-$350. Legs tush
and swing tags were found on this Beanie. This guy was hard to
find starting February of '97, through the scarce spring and summer of '97. Would be a good retirement candidate.
Secondary Market Value: S/S $15-$18
Purchase Date_____ From_____ Price Paid $ _____

Hippity™ the Bunny

Hippity is a cute little bunny
Dressed in green, he looks quite funny
Twitching his nose in the air
Sniffing a flower here and there!

4119   **Hippity the Bunny**   ☐
        CURRENT

COMMENTS: Issued 1997, Birthday 6/1/96, Issue Price $5-$6
Hippity was found with a Bongo swing tag. He would be an excellent choice to have as a McDonald's Teenie Beanie, don't you think? These pastel bunnies are popular ones for the Easter season.

Secondary Market Value: S/S $20-$25

Purchase Date_____ From_____ Price Paid $ _____

_____

_____

Hoot™ the ⊛ Owl

Late to bed, late to rise
Nevertheless, Hoot's quite wise
Studies by candlelight, nothing new
Like a president, do you know Whooo?

4073   **Hoot the Owl**   ☐
          CURRENT
COMMENTS: Issued 1995, Birthday 8/9/95, Issue Price $5-$6
Hoot has been plagued with poem problems such as:
          "Nevertheless, Hoot is qutie wise" instead of "quite."
          "Nevertheless, Hoot's quite wise" instead of "Hoot is..."
The word "sufrace" has been seen on a tush tag. A Zip tag was
found on this wise ole guy! Hoot started to become scarce in
February of '97. As of press time, he still doesn't give a hoot to be
on dealer's shelves! Okay for you, Hoot! It's time for more of you
to fly in! May be a good retirement candidate in the near future.
Secondary Market Value: S/S $12-$14
Purchase Date_____ From_____ Price Paid $ _____

Hoppity™ the Bunny

Hopscotch is what she likes to play
If you don't join in, she'll hop away
So play a game if you have the time,
She likes to play, rain or shine!

4117   Hoppity the Bunny   ☐

CURRENT

COMMENTS: Issued 1997, Birthday 4/3/96, Issue Price $5-$6
Pink Hoppity has been found with two tush tags, also Ears, Mel,
and Ziggy swing tags. Hoppitys must have really been running
around the factory the day of production to get so many tags! This
pink Hoppity seems to be the most scarce of the three pastel
bunnies!

Secondary Market Value: S/S $22-$28

Purchase Date_____ From_____ Price Paid $ _____

Humphrey™ the Camel

4060   Humphrey the Camel

RETIRED 4/96

COMMENTS: Issued 1994, Issue Price $5-$6

Introduced in mid-1994 with a first, second or third generation Ty tag and a black ink body tag. Humphrey is another hard-to-find retired fellow. Note: Humphrey cannot stand by himself! He had a little help from the photographer! Not many folks have Humphrey, but he is probably sitting at the bottom of many toy chests out there! He may be a future garage sale find!

Secondary Market Value: $850-$900

Purchase Date_____ From_____ Price Paid $ _____

Inch™ the Worm

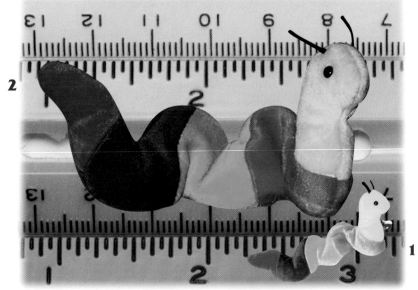

Inch the worm is a friend of mine
He goes so slow all the time
Inching around from here to there
Traveling the world without a care!

4044   **Inch the Worm**   ☐1 ☐2

                CURRENT

COMMENTS: Issued 1995, Birthday 9/3/95, Issue Price $5-$6
He first was found crawling around with a black felt antennae
(Version 1), third generation Ty tag, and a black ink tush tag; he
has gone through a couple of changes. In mid-1996, black yarn
replaced the felt in the antennae and the tags were changed to
fourth generation and red, respectively (Version 2). A very rare find
is a felt antennae and fourth generation tag on this slow fellow. For
Inch with the felt antennae, you will see prices ranging from $95-
$125 on the secondary market. The end of Inch's tail resembles the
color of original Patti the Platypus!

Secondary Market Value: S/S $15-$20

Purchase Date_____ From_____ Price Paid $ _____

_____

_____

Inky™ the ✪Octopus

Inky's head is big and round
As he swims he makes no sound
If you need a hand, don't hesitate
Inky can help because he has eight!

4028   Inky the Octopus   ☐ ☐
                   CURRENT   1   2
COMMENTS: Issued 1994, Birthday 11/29/94, Issue Price $5-$6
Version 1 of Inky had an oval body and is now selling on the secondary market at $300-$325. In mid-1995, the grayish-tan fabric was replaced with pink fabric (Version 2). Production problems include: seven or nine legs instead of eight, and Inky without a mouth (Like ole Spooky). The current, pink Inky has been sought after during the scarce times; there seems to be fewer of this Beanie than most, mainly due to retailers just not ordering him in the past, in my opinion.

Secondary Market Value: S/S $20-$25
Purchase Date_____ From_____ Price Paid $ _____

Jolly™ the Walrus

Jolly the walrus is not very serious
He laughs and laughs until he's delirious
He often reminds me of my dad
Always happy, never sad!

4082   Jolly the Walrus   ☐

CURRENT

COMMENTS: Issued 1997, Birthday 12/2/96, Issue Price $5-$6
Just about the cutest water animal to date. He has a fluffy mustache!

Secondary Market Value: S/S $15-$20

Purchase Date_____ From_____ Price Paid $ _____

_____

_____

Kiwi™ the Toucan

Kiwi waits for the April showers
Watching a garden bloom with flowers
There trees grow with fruit that's sweet
I'm sure you'll guess his favorite treat!

4070   **Kiwi the Toucan**   ☐

RETIRED 1/1/97

COMMENTS: Issued 1995, Birthday 9/16/95, Issue Price $5-$6
Introduced in mid-1995, with third generation Ty tags, Kiwi has
been found missing a toe or having one foot larger than the other.
Tag errors include: two swing tags, a Quackers tush tag, a Scoop,
Seaweed, or Tank swing tag. Kiwi was not a best seller; that, perhaps, led to his retirement, or he may have taken longer to pro-
duce due to his various colors. Display this guy perched in a wire
bird cage. Cute!

Secondary Market Value: $50-$70

Purchase Date_____ From_____ Price Paid $ _____

Lefty™ the Donkey

Donkeys to the left, elephants to the right
Often seems like a crazy sight
This whole game seems very funny
Until you realize they're spending your money!

4085   **Lefty the Donkey**   ☐
          RETIRED 1/1/97
COMMENTS: Issued 1996, Birthday 7/4/96, Issue Price $5-$6
This stubborn blue donkey had many production problems such as:
No flag sewn on, flag sewn on his right side, right ear twice the
size of the left one – add $100; and left ear sewn on backwards –
add $35. Lefty and Righty have become symbols for the two politi-
cal parties. Lefty the Donkey represents the Democratic party.
Righty the Elephant represents the Republican party. Lefty was
very upset when he received a Righty swing tag.
Secondary Market Value: $55-$80
Purchase Date_____ From_____ Price Paid $ _____

Legs™ the Frog

Legs lives in a hollow log
Legs likes to play leap frog
If you like to hang out at the lake
Legs will be the new friend you make!

4020   **Legs the Frog**   ☐
           CURRENT
COMMENTS: Issued 1993, Birthday 4/25/93, Issue Price $5-$6
One of the original nine released in 1993, Legs wears a first generation Ty tag. Production problems include Legs having no tush tag or three legs. Wow, what a hopper! He was found with an Inch swing tag. For the oldest tag expect to pay $25 and up. Frogs are "in." Boys love Legs! Place him on several rocks or looking into a fish bowl for a cute display. Ribbit!
Secondary Market Value: S/S $10-$12
Purchase Date_____ From_____ Price Paid $ _____

Libearty™ the Bear

I am called Libearty
I wear the flag for all to see
Hope and freedom is my way
That's why I wear flag USA!

4057   **Libearty the Bear**   ☐

RETIRED 1/1/97

COMMENTS: Issued 1996, Birthday Summer '96, Issue Price $5-$6
(Pronounced Lă "Bear" tee) Libearty was introduced to commemo-
rate the 1996 Olympics. He was first to carry a star, poem and birth
date tag, along with the fourth generation tag. When first introduced,
his red ink body tag had the word Beanie misspelled as "Beanine."
Not many knew of this error. Production problems include: an upside
down flag, no stitching in face to make it look like "old-face"
Teddy, swing tag which has Valentino, Libearty tush tag, but no
heart or flag, Daisy, Flip, or Valentino tush tag, Nip or Valentino
swing tag. Errors are fun to find and a part of many collectibles!
Secondary Market Value: $65-$85
Purchase Date_____ From_____ Price Paid $ _____

_____

_____

Lizzy™ the Lizard

Her best friend Legs was at her house waiting
Today is the day they go roller blading
But Lizzy Lou had to stay home
So Legs had to roller blade alone.

4033　　　**Lizzy the Lizard**　　　1　2

CURRENT
COMMENTS: Issued 1995, Birthday 5/11/95, Issue Price $5-$6
Alternate poem:
Lizzy loves Legs the frog
She hides with him under logs
Both of them search for flies
Underneath the clear blue skies!

Introduced with the tie-dye fabric, third generation Ty tag, and black ink body tag. This Lizzy sells on the secondary market for $350-$425 (Version 1). Lizzy is currently sporting a bright blue look with black spots on her back, a light to dark yellow underside, third or fourth generation tags and red ink body tags (Version 2). Speedy or Spot swing tags have been found on Lizzy. Lizz the Teenie Beanie was named after Lizzy. Many feel she is a good retirement candidate.

Secondary Market Value: S/S $10-$12

Purchase Date_____ From_____ Price Paid $ _____

_____

_____

Lucky™ the Ladybug

Lucky the ladybug loves the lotto
"Someone must win" that's her motto
But save your dimes and even a penny
Don't spend on the lotto and you'll have many!

4040   Lucky the Ladybug   [1] [2] [3]

CURRENT

COMMENTS: Issued 1994, Birthday 5/1/95, Issue Price $5-$6
Like most ladies, this ladybug cannot make up her mind over what
she wants to wear. In Version 1, she first wore a coat of seven,
9mm, black felt spots glued onto her red back and a second generation Ty tag. The secondary market value of Version 1 is $85-
$100. In Version 2, a change to eleven black spots, which were
part of the fabric, was what this fine lady wore. Finally, Version 3 of
Lucky comes with 21 small, 6mm spots as part of the fabric. She
also has been found with a Bucky tush tag; she just laughed about
that.

Secondary Market Value: S/S $10-$12 (Versions 2 & 3)

Purchase Date_____ From_____ Price Paid $ _____

_____

_____

Magic™ the Dragon

Magic the dragon lives in a dream
The most beautiful that you have ever seen
Through magic lands she likes to fly
Look up and watch her, way up high!

4088　　　　**Magic the Dragon**　　　　1　2
　　　　　　　　CURRENT

COMMENTS: Issued 1995, Birthday 9/5/95, Issue Price $5-$6
Magic first flew into stores with a pale pink thread in her wings
(Version 1). A second version, issued in 1996, displayed hot pink
threads in the wings and is approximately $80-$90 on the secondary market (Version 2). Currently, the wings are back to the
original pale pink thread. Oddities include missing spines, wings
with white or no stitching, and Ears or Gracie tush tags. Very much
sought after during the Spring/early Summer of '97. Good candidate for retirement.

Secondary Market Value: S/S $20-$25

Purchase Date_____ From_____ Price Paid $ _____
_____
_____

Manny™ the Manatee

Manny is sometimes called a sea cow
She likes to twirl and likes to bow
Manny sure is glad you bought her
Because it's so lonely underwater!

4081   Manny the Manatee   ☐
RETIRED 5/11/97
COMMENTS: Issued 1995, Birthday 6/8/95, Issue Price $5-$6
This grey manatee has been found with a poem error such as "like"
instead of "likes." She has been found with a Sting sewn-in tag.
Retirement status is the main reason folks are looking for her. She
was not popular before. Sorry, Manny, but unpopular Beanie
Babies are put out to sea or sent to the jungles.
Secondary Market Value: $45-$65
Purchase Date_____ From_____ Price Paid $ _____

_____

_____

Maple™ the Bear

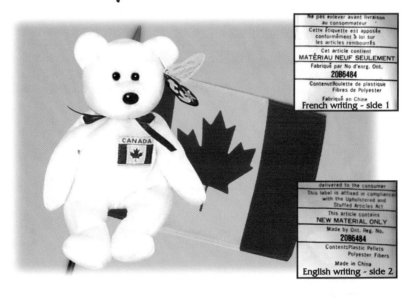

Ne pas enlever avant livraison au consommateur
Cette étiquette est apposée conformément à loi sur les articles rembourrés
Cet article contient
MATÉRIAU NEUF SEULEMENT
Fabriqué par No d'enrg. Ont.
2086484
ContenutBoulette de plastique Fibres de Polyester
Fabriqué en Chine
French writing - side 1

delivered to the consumer
This label is affixed in compliance with the Upholstered and Stuffed Articles Act
This article contains
NEW MATERIAL ONLY
Made by Ont. Reg. No.
2086484
Content:Plastic Pellets Polyester Fibers
Made in China
English writing - side 2

Maple the bear likes to ski
With his friends, he plays hockey.
He loves his pancakes and eats every crumb,
Can you guess which country he's from?

4600   **Maple the Bear**   ☐
          CURRENT

COMMENTS: Issued 1996, Birthday 7/1/96, Issue Price $8-$9
Maple the Bear is a Canadian exclusive and was produced to com-
memorate the Canadian Independence Day. The first 3,000 issued
wore the name "Pride" on their tush tag. Maple with the Pride tush
tag has a secondary market value of $200-$250. With only 3,000
produced, he may go higher. As of June '97, the Maple with the
Maple tush tag debuted in Canada (around 36 per store) and also
began trading on the secondary market almost the same day in the
States. Immediately, this Canadian $8-$9 current bear was selling for
$125 in the United States!! Shown above is a Canadian tush tag.
Secondary Market Value: Maple (Maple tag) –$125
Purchase Date_____ From_____ Price Paid $ _____

Mel™ the Koala

How do you name a Koala bear?
It's rather tough, I do declare!
It confuses me, I get into a funk
I'll name him Mel, after my favorite hunk!

4162　　　**Mel the Koala**　　　☐

CURRENT

COMMENTS: Issued 1997, Birthday 1/15/96, Issue Price $5-$6
Mel was produced to lay on his tummy. Mel has been found with
a Hoppity swing tag, a Scoop tag and a Zip sewn-in tag. Mel
would be a sell-out in Australia, especially in Melbourne. Other
Beanie Companies' Koalas have bushy ears. Not the most popular
in the collection, but he sells eventually...

Secondary Market Value: S/S $15-$20

Purchase Date_____ From_____ Price Paid $ _____

Mystic™ the Unicorn

Once upon a time in a land far away
A baby unicorn was born one day in May
Keep Mystic with you, she's a prize
You'll see the magic in her blue eyes!

4007   **Mystic the Unicorn**   [1] [2]
            CURRENT

COMMENTS: Issued 1994, Birthday 5/21/94, Issue Price $5-$6
Version 1 of Mystic was produced with coarse yarn for the mane
and tail, a second generation Ty tag and a black ink tush tag.
Version 2 was available for six months during '95, with a soft fine
yarn mane and tail. This version has brought $110-$145 on the
secondary market. Considering the limited production time for the
fine yarn mane and tail, I expect this version to go much higher.

Currently, Mystic is back to Version 1. Mystic jumps around
some areas without embroidered nostrils or with short "sprouting
black whiskers" on the left side of her face. Very sought after, even
before the '97 spring scarcity!

Secondary Market Value: S/S $20-$22

Purchase Date_____ From_____ Price Paid $ _____

Nana™ the Monkey

4067   **Nana the Monkey**   ☐
         OUT OF PRODUCTION – NAME CHANGE
COMMENTS: Issued 1995, Birthday 8/17/95, Issue Price $5-$6
What a monkey! Body and tail are the same color. The name was
changed from Nana to Bongo in 1995. See page 8 for Bongo.
Secondary Market Value: $650-$750
Purchase Date_____ From_____ Price Paid $ _____
_____
_____

Nanook™ the Husky

Nanook is a dog that loves cold weather
To him a sled is light as a feather
Over the snow and through the slush
He runs at hearing the cry of "mush!"

4104   **Nanook the Husky**   ☐
         CURRENT
COMMENTS: Issued 1997, Birthday 11/21/96, Issue Price $5-$6
Nanook mushes through some blizzards with a Ringo tush tag. A
cute li'l fellow. Secondary market dealers had many during the
scarce time and they were reselling them for $15-$20 very
quickly.
Secondary Market Value: S/S $15-$20
Purchase Date_____ From_____ Price Paid $ _____

Nip™ the Cat

His name is Nipper, but we call him Nip
His best friend is a black cat named Zip
Nip likes to run in races for fun
He runs so fast he's always number one!

4003   **Nip the Cat**   ☐1 ☐2 ☐3
            CURRENT
COMMENTS: Issued 1994, Birthday 3/6/94, Issue Price $5-$6
The Version 1 Nip was larger with a white triangle on his face and
a white belly. He was released with second and third generation
Ty tags. Value him at $175-$200. Version 2 Nip is more scarce.
This Nip is all one color, with the exception of pink on the inside of
the ears and pink whiskers. He has third generation tags and the
earlier black ink tush tag. A value of $650-$750 is common on the
secondary market for Version 2 Nip. Currently, Version 3 Nip has a
smaller gold body, white paws, a pink nose, white ears and
whiskers. Good retirement candidate.
Secondary Market Value: S/S $10-$12
Purchase Date_____ From_____ Price Paid $ _____

Nuts™ the Squirrel

With his bushy tail, he'll scamper up a tree
The most cheerful critter you'll ever see,
He's nuts about nuts, and he loves to chat
Have ever seen a squirrel like that?

4114   **Nuts the Squirrel**   ☐
        CURRENT
COMMENTS: Issued 1997, Birthday 1/21/96, Issue Price $5-$6
Nuts scampers to some collectors with continuous loops of
whiskers as the yarn is left uncut. At times he has been found with
no whiskers at all. Nuts has also been seen scampering around
with his tail not sewn up his back properly, light beige belly
extending up to the nose and with eyes on differently so that he's
looking up, not at you. Hippity sewn-in tags have been found on
Nuts as well. Quite a character!
Secondary Market Value: S/S $10-$12
Purchase Date_____ From_____ Price Paid $ _____

Patti™ the Platypus

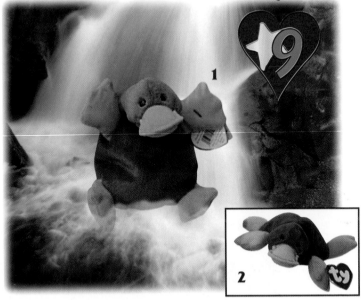

1

2

Ran into Patti one day while walking
Believe me she wouldn't stop talking
Listened and listened to her speak
That would explain her extra large beak!

4025   **Patti the Platypus**   [1] [2]

CURRENT

COMMENTS: Issued 1993, Birthday 1/6/93, Issue Price $5-$6
One of the original nine released in '93, Patti was first introduced
with a color resembling the fabric in Teddy the Magenta Bear
(Version 1). Patti with this coloring is approximately $600-$610 on
the secondary market! Version 2 had a purple hue which closely
resembles the color of Inch the Inchworm's tail. Patti also became
a McDonald's Teenie Beanie! A retirement candidate, in my opinion.

Secondary Market Value: S/S $10-$12

Purchase Date_____ From_____ Price Paid $ _____

Peace™ the Bear

4053   Peace the Bear

CURRENT

COMMENTS: Issued 1997, Birthday 2/1/96, Issue Price $5-$6
This bear truly is a peace loving fellow. Notice the peace symbol
on his chest, for example. (At press time, this bear was unavail-
able. The artwork pictured resembles Peace, as pictured on Ty's
Web site.) Rumored in June, a Teenie Beanie Peace was
"accidently" given out at a McDonald's.

Secondary Market Value: Not established

Purchase Date_____ From_____ Price Paid $ _____

_____

_____

Peanut™ the Elephant

Peanut the elephant walks on tip-toes
Quietly sneaking wherever she goes
She'll sneak up on you and a hug you will get
Peanut is a friend you won't soon forget!

4062　　　**Peanut the Elephant**　　　１　２

CURRENT

COMMENTS: Issued 1995, Birthday 1/25/95, Issue Price $5-$6
There was only one royal blue Peanut shipment in July, 1995.
Peanut was valued from $1,500-$2,000 as of mid-1997 (Version
1). Will she go higher? Time will tell. I did see two royal blue
Peanuts sell for $1,500 and $2,000, respectively, at one of my
annual Beanie Swap Meets. Remember that the royal blue Peanut
did not come with the fourth generation Ty tag. Currently, Peanut
is light blue (Version 2). She has been found with an errored tag
such as a Bones tush tag or a Tank swing tag.
Secondary Market Value: S/S $10-$12
Purchase Date_____ From_____ Price Paid $ _____

Peking™ the Panda

4013   **Peking the Panda**   ☐
            RETIRED 4/96
COMMENTS: Issued 1994, Issue Price $5-$6
Originally produced to lay on his tummy, Peking is a very rare
panda bear. Even more rare is the oddity of one brown and one
black eye that was reported. This panda bears a third generation Ty
tag and is not easily found.
Secondary Market Value: $550-$675
Purchase Date_____ From_____ Price Paid $ _____
_____
_____

Pinchers™ the Lobster

This lobster loves to pinch
Eating his food inch by inch
Balancing carefully with his tail
Moving forward slow as a snail!

4026   **Pinchers the Lobster**   ☐

CURRENT

COMMENTS: Issued 1993, Birthday 6/19/93, Issue Price $5-$6
One of the original nine, Pinchers has a first generation Ty tag.
Several swing tags had errors such as a Patti swing tag and a
Mystic or Speedy sewn-in tag. A "Punchers" swing tag has also
been reported. However, the Ty company will not confirm at this
time that "Punchers" was ever produced with a name change to
Pinchers, as in the case of Nana changing to Bongo. At this time
insure Pinchers with a "Punchers" swing tag for at least $300. A
good retirement candidate!
Secondary Market Value: S/S $10-$12
Purchase Date_____ From_____ Price Paid $ _____

Pinky™ the Flamingo

Pinky loves the Everglades
From the hottest pink she's made
With floppy legs and big orange beak
She's the Beanie that you seek!

4072　　　　**Pinky the Flamingo**　　　　☐
　　　　　　CURRENT
COMMENTS: Issued 1995, Birthday 2/13/95, Issue Price $5-$6
Now you no longer have to travel to Florida to see one of these
beautiful creatures. "Odd" Pinkys include one wing sewn on
upside-down: top of one is light, top of other is dark. Chops tush
tags have been found occasionally on Pinky. She was very scarce
last winter and spring of '97. A Teenie Beanie Baby named Pinky
debuted with the April '97 McDonald's promotion.
Secondary Market Value: S/S $12-$15
Purchase Date_____ From_____ Price Paid $ _____

Pouch™ the Kangaroo

My little pouch is handy I've found
It helps me carry my baby around
I hop up and down without any fear
Knowing my baby is safe and near.

4161　　　　**Pouch the Kangaroo**　　　　☐
　　　　　　CURRENT
COMMENTS: Issued 1997, Birthday 11/6/96, Issue Price $5-$6
Errored tags found on Pouch include a Bones swing tags, Gracie
and Valentino tush tags. Some say they don't care for only the
joey's head in mom's pouch. I assume a complete sized joey
would cause major changes and increase the cost. Be happy for
now!
Secondary Market Value: S/S $12-$15
Purchase Date_____ From_____ Price Paid $ _____

Kids' Day at Rosie's Posies

Beanie Babies™ are collected by children!

During the Scarce Summer of '97, Beanie Babies were very hard to find. This scarcity prompted Rosie to hold a Kids' Day at her store.

A Happy Group Looking In Rosie's Window

Above: Garcia drawn by Brittany E.

Below: Garcia drawn by Jasmine T.

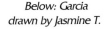

Children, alone, were allowed in the store to purchase that extra-special Beanie Baby that they had been wishing for...

Happy the Clown performed outside to entertain those who were waiting at Rosie's Posies in Canton, IL. No adults were allowed into the store unless they were accompanied by a child age four or under. The children were limited to two Beanie Babies so there would be enough for each of the 300 children who attended.

In addition, a coloring contest was held. Shown are a few of the the winners.

Right: Blizzard the Tiger drawn by Brandon E.

73

Pugsly™ the Pug

Pugsly is picky about what he will wear
Never a spot, a stain or a tear
Image is something of which he'll gloat
Until he noticed his wrinkled coat!

4106   **Pugsly the Pug**   ☐

           CURRENT

COMMENTS: Issued 1997, Birthday 5/2/96, Issue Price $5-$6
You li'l ugly dog… you're cute!
Secondary Market Value: S/S $15-$20
Purchase Date_____ From_____ Price Paid $ _____

_____

_____

Quackers™ the Duck

There is a duck by the name of Quackers
Every night he eats animal crackers
He swims in a lake that's clear and blue
But he'll come to the shore to be with you!

4024   **Quackers the Duck**   ☐1 ☐2

        CURRENT

COMMENTS: Issued 1994, Birthday 4/19/94, Issue Price $5-$6
Quackers is no ugly duckling! Version 1 had no wings and has a
secondary market value of $1,000-$1,500. Old tags have been
found that say "Quacker." Currently, Quackers comes complete
with wings (Version 2). Quacks the Teenie Beanie seemed to be
more abundant than other Teenies at McDonald's.

Secondary Market Value: S/S $10-$12

Purchase Date_____ From_____ Price Paid $ _____

Radar™ the Bat

Radar the bat flies late at night
He can soar to an amazing height
If you see something as high as a star
Take a good look, it might be Radar!

4091   **Radar the Bat**   ☐
        RETIRED 5/11/97
COMMENTS: Issue 1995, Birthday 10/30/95, Issue Price $5-$6
It's a bird; it's a plane; no, it's Radar the Bat! Oddities on this creature include only one foot, one eye or one foot half the size of the
other. Tags with errors are common with Radar. It seems when he
was available in '95 through '97, he just didn't sell well and retailers did not reorder. Thus, he became harder to find before retirement.
Secondary Market Value: $75-$85
Purchase Date_____ From_____ Price Paid $ _____

Rex™ the Tyrannosaurus

4086   **Rex the Tyrannosaurus**   ☐
             RETIRED 4/96
COMMENTS: Issued 1995, Issue Price $5-$6
Now stomping with his fellow dinosaurs in retirement, Rex wore
the third generation Ty tag. When Rex roamed the earth, Beanie
Babies were not quite as collectible as today, so these are more
scarce on the secondary market than today's retired characters.
Secondary Market Value: $250-$285
Purchase Date_____ From_____ Price Paid $ _____

_____

_____

Righty™ the Elephant

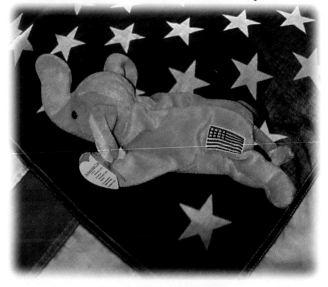

Donkeys to the left, elephants to the right
Often seems like a crazy sight
This whole game seems very funny
Until you realize they're spending your money!

4086　　　　**Righty the Elephant**　　　　☐

RETIRED 1/1/97

COMMENTS: Issued 1996, Birthday 7/4/96, Issue Price $5-$6
For many, Righty the Elephant symbolizes the Republican Party
with the American flag sewn on. Of course, oddities such as the
flag being upside down or no flag at all have appeared. Freckles,
Quackers, and Waddle tags have been found on this elephant.
Righty is not as much in demand as Lefty the Donkey for some
unknown reason. Perhaps elephants sold better so retailers
ordered more than the Donkeys. Expect these values to increase
to at least $95 by late '97 - early '98.
Secondary Market Value: $60-$75
Purchase Date_____ From_____ Price Paid $ _____

Ringo™ the Raccoon

Ringo hides behind his mask
He will come out, if you should ask
He loves to chitter, he loves to chatter
Just about anything, it doesn't matter!

4014   **Ringo the Raccoon**   ☐
              CURRENT
COMMENTS: Issued 1995, Birthday 7/14/95, Issue Price $5-$6
Oops… Poor ole Ringo was found without eyes! He's a popular ole
guy. Doodle, the Rooster crossed the road to show Ringo "it can
be done!" (That was a joke - get it?)
Secondary Market Value: S/S $12-$14
Purchase Date_____ From_____ Price Paid $ _____
_____
_____

Roary™ the Lion

Deep in the jungle they crowned him king
But being brave is not his thing
A cowardly lion some may say
He hears his roar and runs away!

4069   **Roary the Lion**   ☐
                    CURRENT
COMMENTS: Issued 1997, Birthday 2/20/96, Issue Price $5-$6
As of early July '97, many retailers had not even received him!
Retailers sold these, as well as the other current Beanie Babies, at
retail up to $12.95, several at $19.95! In large malls in St. Louis,
where I purchased several "older" current Beanie Babies, $8.99
was the norm. The S/S period was a rough time for Beanie Babies
folk!
Secondary Market Value: S/S $18-$20
Purchase Date_____ From_____ Price Paid $ _____
_____
_____

Rover™ the Dog

This dog is red and his name is Rover
If you call him he is sure to come over
He barks and plays with all his might
But worry not, he won't bite!

4101   **Rover the Dog**   ☐

> *CURRENT*

COMMENTS: Issued 1996, Birthday 5/30/96, Issue Price $5-$6
Sparky and Waddle swing tags have been found on this frolicking
pup. Rover is a fourth generation Ty tagged dog. Rover would
make an excellent Teenie Beanie for a McDonald's promotion if
there is another one. Time will tell. Rover looks great with a black
collar.

Secondary Market Value: S/S $10-$12

Purchase Date_____ From_____ Price Paid $ _____

Scoop™ the Pelican

All day long he scoops up fish
To fill his bill, is his wish
Diving fast and diving low
Hoping those fish are very slow!

4107   **Scoop the Pelican**   ☐
            CURRENT
COMMENTS: Issued 1996, Birthday 7/1/96, Issue Price $5-$6
Scoop him up into your heart! Oddities include a white patch of
material attached to the bottom of his beak and various errors on
his tag. There is talk of retirement due to his size and the fact that
he is not as popular as other Beanies. He should be displayed with
the Ty fish, his buddies!
Secondary Market Value: S/S $10-$12
Purchase Date_____ From_____ Price Paid $ _____

Scottie™ the Scottish Terrier

Scottie is a friendly sort
Even though his legs are short
He is always happy as can be
His best friends are you and me!

4102   **Scottie the Scottish Terrier**   ☐

CURRENT

COMMENTS: Issued 1995, Birthday 6/15/96, Issue Price $5-$6
A soft, nappy fabric covers this black terrier. Check his swing tag
for a misprinted birthdate of 6/3/96 or "slways" instead of
"always" in the poem. Floppity, Freckles or Velvet tush tags as well
as a Wrinkles swing tag have been discovered on this fourth generation tagged Beanie Baby. He needs a red collar to spruce him
up! A great retirement candidate!

Secondary Market Value: S/S $10-$12

Purchase Date_____ From_____ Price Paid $ _____

Seamore™ the Seal

Seamore is a little white seal
Fish and clams are her favorite meal
Playing and laughing in the sand
She's the happiest seal in the land!

4029   Seamore the Seal   ☐

CURRENT

COMMENTS: Issued 1995, Birthday 12/14/96, Issue Price $5-$6
Digger, Inky, Kiwi and Legs tush and swing tags have been found
on this white seal. Seamore, the Teenie Beanie, is a close friend of
the older Seamore the Seal. A popular gal!

Secondary Market Value: S/S $10-$12

Purchase Date_____ From_____ Price Paid $ _____

_____

_____

Seaweed™ the ✪tter

Seaweed is what she like to eat
It's supposed to be a delicious treat
Have you tried a treat from the water
If you haven't, maybe you "otter"!

4080   **Seaweed the Otter**   ☐
        CURRENT

COMMENTS: Issued 1996, Birthday 3/19/96, Issue Price $5-$6
Otter, Otter everywhere and not a pond lily to eat...
Oddities such as an inside-out sewn-in tag and various other
errored tags were found on this girl. She's really a super gal and
designed somewhat differently so she may relax ands swim on her
back, which is quite natural for her.
Secondary Market Value: S/S $10-$12
Purchase Date_____ From_____ Price Paid $ _____

_____

_____

Slither™ the Snake

4031   **Slither the Snake**   ☐

RETIRED 4/96

COMMENTS: Issued 1994, Issue Price $5-$6

Sssssss... Try to find him if you can. He's 23" long! I personally saw two of these guys sell in March of '97 at $400 each. Slither is just not easy to find!

Secondary Market Value: $450-$500

Purchase Date_____ From_____ Price Paid $ _____

Sly™ the Fox

Sly is a fox and tricky is he
Please don't chase him, let him be
If you want him just say when
He'll peek out from his den!

4115   **Sly the Fox**   ☐
                CURRENT

COMMENTS: Issued 1996, Birthday 9/12/96, Issue Price $5-$6
Sly was first released with an all brown body and white fabric
inside his dark brown ears and on his lower muzzle area. His secondary market value is $60-$80. He has a red ink body tag.
Currently, this fourth generation tagged fox sports a white underbelly. He has been found with either a Congo sewn-in, Tabasco
sewn-in or Pinky swing tag. Sly says he's been hoping you'll display him by Doodle - Hee, hee! Sly heard Doodle could get a
name change - time will tell...
Secondary Market Value: S/S $10-$12
Purchase Date_____ From_____ Price Paid $ _____

Snip™ the Siamese Cat

Snip the cat is Siamese
She'll be your friend if you please
So toss her a toy or piece of string
Playing with you is her favorite thing!

4120   **Snip the Siamese Cat**   ☐
            CURRENT
COMMENTS: Issued 1997, Birthday 10/22/96, Issue Price $5-$6
Some Snips arrived without whiskers! She has been found with a
Grunt, Nuts or Zip tush tag or a Snort or Wrinkles tag.
Secondary Market Value: S/S $15-$20
Purchase Date_____ From_____ Price Paid $ _____

_____

_____

Snort™ the Bull

Although Snort is not so tall
He loves to play basketball
He is a star player in his dream
Can you guess his favorite team?

4002   **Snort the Bull**   ☐

CURRENT

COMMENTS: Issued 1996, Birthday 5/15/96, Issue Price $5-$6
Revised from Tabasco the Bull to have cream colored hooves,
Snort has been found with one of his ears sewn on backwards.
Snort's errored tags include no tush tag, a Sparky tush tag or a
Tabasco or Hoot swing tag. A Snort with a Tabasco swing tag has
sold for up to $40. Some folks have been buying Snort with a
Tabasco tag and then replacing it on a Tabasco that had a lost tag.
Snort is really popular with the Bulls fans! Another "Bull" produced
was Snort the Teenie Beanie!

Secondary Market Value: S/S $12-$15

Purchase Date_____ From_____ Price Paid $ _____

Sparky™ the Dalmatian

Sparky rides proud on the fire truck
Ringing the bell and pushing his luck
He gets under foot when trying to help
He often gets stepped on and lets out a yelp!

4100   **Sparky the Dalmatian**   ☐
          RETIRED 5/11/97

COMMENTS: Issued 1996, Birthday 2/27/96, Issue Price $5-$6
Sparky the Dalmatian has been found romping with different last
poem lines:

"He often "get" stepped on..."
"He often gets stepped on crying yelp!"
"... step on him and he will let out a yelp!"

He also searches for fires with Bubbles or Rover tush tags or Magic
or Wrinkles swing tags. Sparky was scarce before the "real" scarcity of '97. By mid-1998, Sparky may be up to $65.
Secondary Market Value: $40-$45

Purchase Date_____ From_____ Price Paid $ _____

Speedy™ the Turtle

Speedy ran marathons in the past
Such a shame, always last
Now Speedy is a bright star
After he bought a racing car!

4030   **Speedy the Turtle**   ☐

CURRENT

COMMENTS: Issued 1994, Birthday 8/14/94, Issue Price $5-$6
Speedy crawls through some races with a Legs tush tag. It doesn't
seem to have affected his speed at all! He could get retired if a
different sea turtle would replace him... Speedy also appears as a
Teenie Beanie Baby.

Secondary Market Value: S/S $10-$12

Purchase Date_____ From_____ Price Paid $ _____

Spike™ the Rhinoceros

Spike the rhino likes to stampede
He's the bruiser that you need
Gentle to birds on his back and spike
You can be his friend if you like!

4060   **Spike the Rhinoceros**   ☐
          CURRENT
COMMENTS: Issued 1996, Birthday 8/13/96, Issue Price $5-$6
Would you believe Tabasco's tush tag appeared on this character
as well as Spooky's swing tag?! Hey! We don't want this guy
gettin' mad! CHARGE! Spike is a good candidate for retirement.
Secondary Market Value: S/S $10-$12
Purchase Date_____ From_____ Price Paid $ _____

_____

_____

Splash™ the ☆Orca Whale

Splash loves to jump and dive
He's the fastest whale alive
He always wins the 100 yard dash
With a victory jump he'll make a splash!

4022   **Splash the Orca Whale**   ☐
          RETIRED 5/11/97
COMMENTS: Issued 1993, Birthday 7/8/93, Issue Price $5-$6
Splash arrived with the original nine in 1993. His tag was a first
generation Ty tag.
Secondary Market Value: $50-$60
Purchase Date_____ From_____ Price Paid $ _____

_____

_____

Spooky™ the Ghost

Ghosts can be a scary sight
But don't let Spooky bring you any fright
Because when you're alone, you will see
The best friend that Spooky can be!

4090   **Spooky the Ghost**   ☐
           CURRENT

COMMENTS: Issued 1995, Birthday 10/31/95, Issue Price $5-$6
This Halloween ghost began his haunt with the name of "Spook," a
third generation tag and a black ink body tag on his side. The tag
also carries the designer's name under the style number on the
third generation tag, but not on the fourth. He has been found
with three arms, a swing tag that reads "Spook" instead of
Spooky, and Ringo or Wrinkles tush tags. Three mouth styles exist
for Spooky: V-shape (far left photo), full-smile (center photo) and a
half-smile (far right photo). Insure "Spook" for $175-$200. Spooky
was scarce throughout winter of '96 and on through the summer
of '97.
Secondary Market Value: S/S $20-$35
Purchase Date_____ From_____ Price Paid $ _____

Spot™ the Dog

See Spot sprint, see Spot run
You and Spot will have lots of fun
Watch out now, because he's not slow
Just stand back and watch him go!

4000   **Spot the Dog**   ☐1 ☐2

CURRENT

COMMENTS: Issued 1993, Birthday 1/3/93, Issue Price $5-$6
One of the first nine released in 1993, Spot originally did not have
a black spot on his back! His tag was a first generation Ty tag. He
has been found without the black spot on the left side of his face
or with a white tail versus the more common black tail. Spot without the spot on his back is valued at $1,000-$1,250 at sales. Spot
is a good candidate for retirement!

Secondary Market Value: S/S $10-$12

Purchase Date_____ From_____ Price Paid $ _____

Squealer™ the Pig

Squealer likes to joke around
He is known as class clown
Listen to his stories for a while
There is no doubt he will make you smile!

4005   **Squealer the Pig**   ☐

   CURRENT

COMMENTS: Issued 1993, Birthday 4/23/93, Issue Price $5-$6
Another member of the original nine, Squealer sneaks around with
a first generation Ty tag. He has been found with a Blackie tush tag
and a Bucky swing tag. Poem errors include "Squealer like to joke
around" and "There is no doubt he'll will make you smile!"
Secondary Market Value: S/S $10-$12

Purchase Date_____ From_____ Price Paid $ _____

_____

_____

Steg™ the Stegosaurus

4087   **Steg the Stegosaurus**   ☐
               RETIRED 4/96
COMMENTS: Issued 1995, Issue Price $5-$6
This member of the tie-dye dinosaur collection wore the third generation Ty tag before retirement. Not easy to locate – many current sales found from $185-$200. I expect his value to increase 10-20% in '98, as the Beanie Babies trend continues.
Secondary Market Value: $225-$240
Purchase Date_____ From_____ Price Paid $ _____

_____

_____

Sting™ the Stingray

I'm a manta ray and my name is Sting
I'm quite unusual and this is the thing
Under the water I glide like a bird
Have you ever seen something so absurd?

4077　　　**Sting the Stingray**　　　☐
RETIRED 1/1/97
COMMENTS: Issued 1995, Birthday 8/27/95, Issue Price $5-$6
Sting debuted with a third generation Ty tag and a black ink tush
tag, originally. By mid-1996, Sting was retagged with the fourth
generation Ty tag and the red ink tush tag. Sting has been occasionally tagged in error with a Pouch, Ringo, Tank or Valentino tush
tag. Sting was not a popular guy, so he met his Waterloo! Retired!
Secondary Market Value: $60-$80
Purchase Date_____ From_____ Price Paid $ _____

Stinky™ the Skunk

Deep in the woods he lived in a cave
Perfume and mints were the gifts they gave
He showered every night in the kitchen sink
Hoping one day he wouldn't stink!

4017   **Stinky the Skunk**   ☐
         CURRENT
COMMENTS: Issued 1995, Birthday 2/13/95, Issue Price $5-$6
Skunks are always overwhelming! Stinky is no exception, with his
Bongo and Radar tush tags and Congo and Zip swing tags appear-
ing on various pieces.
Secondary Market Value: S/S $10-$12
Purchase Date_____ From_____ Price Paid $ _____

_____

_____

Stripes™ the Tiger

1   3   2

Stripes was never fierce nor strong
So with tigers, he didn't get along
Jungle life was hard to get by
So he came to his friends at Ty!

4065   **Stripes the Tiger**   1 2 3
          CURRENT

COMMENTS: Issued 1995, Birthday 6/11/95, Issue Price $5-$6
Version 1 Stripes first pounced into production with darker colored
orange fabric, and closely placed stripes. He was also produced
with a thicker, more plush fabric as in Version 2. This darker colored Version 1 and Version 2 secondary market price is from $140-
$175. With the new fourth generation tags came a new lighter
orange color and fewer stripes (Version 3). Poems have read
"Jungle life was hard getting by" compared to the correct poem
which reads "Jungle life was hard to get by." Both versions of
Stripe have been found with errored tags.
Secondary Market Value: S/S $12-$14
Purchase Date_____ From_____ Price Paid $ _____

Tabasco™ the Bull

Although Tabasco is not so tall
He loves to play basketball
He is a star player in his dream
Can you guess his favorite team?

4002   **Tabasco the Bull**   ☐
                  RETIRED 1/97
COMMENTS: Issued 1995, Birthday 5/15/95, Issue Price $5-$6
Tabasco was possibly retired because of the name associated with
the Tabasco Company. Tabasco the Bull has been found with no
stitches on the nostrils, only one horn and even one with only one
eye. Errored tags such as Lefty, Spike, Snort or Grunt appear on
Tabasco. There were approximately three million produced! He is
the most talked about Beanie Baby by those who do not even col-
lect. His poem mentions basketball and many thought he was a
Chicago Bulls fan!
Secondary Market Value: $200-$250
Purchase Date_____ From_____ Price Paid $ _____

Tank™ the Armadillo

This armadillo lives in the South
Shoving Tex-Mex in his mouth
He sure loves it south of the border
Keeping his friends in good order!

4031   **Tank the Armadillo**   ① ② ③

CURRENT

COMMENTS: Issued 1995, Birthday 2/22/95, Issue Price $5-$6
Tank has slowly rumbled around in three different coats of armor.
In Version 1, he first had more beans, seven sewn-in body plates, a
third generation Ty tag, and red ink body tag. Insure this Tank for
$75-$80. In 1996, He was released with a fourth generation Ty
tag, two more sewn body plates (total of nine), and a red ink tag
(Version 2). This Version 2 Tank is worth around $90-$110 on the
secondary market. Finally, in late 1996, he settled with a slightly
smaller body with nine body plates and a horizontal sewn in line
which runs along the bottom of the nine body plates (Version 3).
His poem occasionally reads "boarder" instead of "border." Few
armadillo toys or plush animals are produced, so he is definitely a
great find!

Secondary Market Value: S/S $10-$12

Purchase Date_____ From_____ Price Paid $ _____

Teddy™ the Bear

Teddy wanted to go out today
All of his friends went out to play
But he'd rather help whatever you do
After all, his best friend is you!

4050   **Teddy the Bear**   1 2
                      CURRENT

COMMENTS: Issued 1994, Birthday 11/28/95, Issue Price $5-$6
Originally introduced with a narrow European style face (Version
1), first and second generation Ty tag, eyes placed to the side and
smaller nose, he changed to a newer look wearing a second and
third generation tag and a burgundy ribbon around his neck
(Version 2). Blank swing tags have been found. Teddy's older,
European style is valued at $650-$700.
Secondary Market Value: S/S $12-$14
Purchase Date_____ From_____ Price Paid $ _____
_____
_____

Teddy™ the Cranberry Bear

2

1

4052	**Teddy the Cranberry Bear**	① ②

RETIRED 4/96

COMMENTS: Issued 1994, Issue Price $5-$6

Teddy the Cranberry bear came with first and second generation Ty tags with the smaller Ty lettering on both the single and double tags, the European style face, smaller nose, and eyes on the side (Version 1). His newer look included a green ribbon and second or third generation tags (Version 2). On the European market, the older European style Teddys were readily found. As Europeans did not prefer the colored bears over Teddy Brown, they did not buy as many. Many of the bigger secondary market dealers were able to go to Europe and buy the leftovers. Thus, there was an ample supply in the States. This explains why, currently, the price for the older colored teddy bears is less than the new, despite both being retired. For example, old Teddy Cranberry (Version 1) is worth $425-$500 and the secondary market value shown below is for Version 2.

Secondary Market Value: $500-$550

Purchase Date_____ From_____ Price Paid $ _____

Teddy™ the Jade Bear

4057   **Teddy the Jade Bear**   1 2
RETIRED 4/96
COMMENTS: Issued 1994, Issue Price $5-$6
The narrow European style face and first or second generation Ty tags came with the original Teddy the Jade Bear (Version 1). His second look had the addition of a maroon ribbon and second or third generation tags (Version 2). The Version 1 Teddy Jade is valued at around $250-$300. These "colored" bears are gorgeous! More colored bears please, Mr. Ty!
Secondary Market Value: $500-$525
Purchase Date_____ From_____ Price Paid $ _____

Teddy™ the Magenta Bear

4056   **Teddy the Magenta Bear**   1 2
                  RETIRED 4/96

COMMENTS: Issued 1994, Issue Price $5-$6

The addition of a colored ribbon around Teddy Magenta's neck and a facelift (Version 2) replaced the original European style (Version 1). The Version 1 Teddy Magenta should be insured for $350-$385. There are currently many reports that the new face Teddy Magenta is selling for around $500-$525 on the secondary market. Look for price to possibly increase to $550-$600 in '98! Gorgeous!

Secondary Market Value: $500-$550

Purchase Date_____ From_____ Price Paid $ _____

Teddy™ the Teal Bear

4051   **Teddy the Teal Bear**   1 2

RETIRED 4/96

COMMENTS: Issued 1994, Issue Price $5-$6

Originally "bearing" the European style teddy bear face (Version 1), Teddy Teal decided on a new look. Teddy Teal wears a "berry" blue ribbon around his neck on Version 2. The Version 1 Teddy Teal ranges from $350-$400 on the secondary market. These colored bears are G-R-E-A-T!

Secondary Market Value: $680-$750

Purchase Date_____ From_____ Price Paid $ _____

_____

_____

Teddy™ the Violet Bear

4055   **Teddy the Violet Bear**   1   2
                    RETIRED 4/96
COMMENTS: Issued 1994, Issue Price $5-$6
After the change from a European face (Version 1), Teddy Violet
sports a green ribbon (Version 2). Version 1's value on the sec-
ondary market is $325-$375. Oh, so nice! Teddy Violet is on
everyone's wish list!
Secondary Market Value: $700-$750
Purchase Date_____ From_____ Price Paid $ _____

_____

_____

Trap™ the Mouse

4042   **Trap the Mouse**   ☐

RETIRED 4/96

COMMENTS: Issued 1994, Issue Price $5-$6

Introduced with the first generation single Ty tags, Trap later acquired the second generation tag and, with his retirement, had the third generation tag. All had a black ink tush tag. He's been found with three legs... there must have been a mouse trap around, or a slow hawk! Ouch!

Secondary Market Value: $400-$450

Purchase Date_____ From_____ Price Paid $ _____

Tuffy™ the Terrier

Taking off with a thunderous blast
Tuffy rides his motorcycle fast
The Beanies roll with laughs & squeals
He never took off his training wheels!

4108 **Tuffy the Terrier** ☐

CURRENT

COMMENTS: Issued 1997, Birthday 10/12/96, Issue Price $5-$6
This tough guy wears a coat of nappy fabric instead of the normal plush. Pretty cute...

Secondary Market Value: S/S $15-$20

Purchase Date_____ From_____ Price Paid $ _____

_____

_____

Tusk™ the Walrus

Tusk brushes his teeth everyday
To keep them shiny, it's the only way
Teeth are special, so you must try
So they sparkle when you say "Hi"!

4076 **Tusk the Walrus** ☐
RETIRED 1/1/97
COMMENTS: Issued 1994, Birthday 9/18/95, Issue Price $5-$6
Known also under the alias of "Tuck" (errored swing tag). Early
shipments of Tusk carried up-turned tusks. Variations include back-
ward and downward facing tusks, a swing tag mistake of "sufrace,"
and, in the last line of the poem, an error that reads, "And they
will sparkle when you say 'Hi'!" and various tagging errors have
shown up as well. "Tuck" is valued at $60-$65 on the secondary
market!
Secondary Market Value: $55-$60
Purchase Date_____ From_____ Price Paid $ _____

Twigs™ the Giraffe

Twigs has his head in the clouds
He stands tall, he stands proud
With legs so skinny they wobble and shake
What an unusual friend he will make!

4068   **Twigs the Giraffe**   ☐
                  CURRENT

COMMENTS: Issued 1995, Birthday 5/19/95, Issue Price $5-$6
Bongo and Weenie tush tags have been found on this tall creature.
In late winter of '96 he was scarce, as well as in the following
summer! I would assume this material is not produced in large
quantity, thus perhaps a wait is required to get Twigs produced.
Secondary Market Value: S/S $12-$14
Purchase Date_____ From_____ Price Paid $ _____

_____

_____

Valentino™ the Bear

His heart is red and full of love
He cares for you so give him a hug
Keep him close when feeling blue
Feel the love he has for you!

4058   **Valentino the Bear**   ☐
                      CURRENT

COMMENTS: Issued 1994, Birthday 2/14/94, Issue Price $5-$6
The red heart on his chest reminds us that his birthday is on
Valentine's Day. Variations, such as one eye smaller in size,
appeared on this third and fourth generation Ty-tagged bear. He
was scarce even before the Spring and Summer of '97! May be a
good retirement candidate.
Secondary Market Value: S/S $18-$25
Purchase Date_____ From_____ Price Paid $ _____

Velvet™ the Panther

Velvet loves to sleep in the trees
Lulled to dreams by the buzz of the bees
She snoozes all day and plays all night
Running and jumping in the moonlight!

4064 **Velvet the Panther** ☐

CURRENT

COMMENTS: Issued 1995, Birthday 12/16/95, Issue Price $5-$6
This black beauty lunges around with a few errored swing tags:
Grunt, Hoppity and Wrinkle. Freckles, Quacker and Seaweed tush
tags have also popped up on Velvet. This is the little boys' favorite
of the cat family! A popular panther!

Secondary Market Value: S/S $10-$15

Purchase Date_____ From_____ Price Paid $ _____

Waddle™ the Penguin

Waddle the Penguin likes to dress up
Every night he wears his tux
When Waddle walks, it never fails
He always trips over his tails!

4075   **Waddle the Penguin**   ☐
    CURRENT
COMMENTS: Issued 1995, Birthday 12/19/95, Issue Price $5-$6
Here's a bird who cannot fly!
Secondary Market Value: S/S $10-$12
Purchase Date_____ From_____ Price Paid $ _____

Waves™ the ✪rca Whale

Join him today on the Internet
Don't be afraid to get your feet wet
He taught all the Beanies how to surf
Our web page is his home turf!

4084   **Waves the Orca Whale**   ☐
          CURRENT
COMMENTS: Issued 1997, Birthday 12/8/96, Issue Price $5-$6
Waves says to display him in an aquarium (no water please!) along
with Waves, Crunch, and Bubbles! Waves was disappointed that
Echo's swing tag was found on him when he debuted.
Secondary Market Value: S/S $15-$20
Purchase Date_____ From_____ Price Paid $ _____

Web™ the Spider

4041   **Web the Spider**   ☐
          RETIRED 7/96
COMMENTS: Issued 1994, Issue Price $5-$6
Web easily catches flies in his third generation Ty tag, black tush
tag and his neatly designed web! Not owned by many...
Secondary Market Value: $450-$500
Purchase Date_____ From_____ Price Paid $ _____

Weenie™ the Dog

Weenie the dog is quite a sight.
Long of body and short of height
He perches himself high on a log
And considers himself to be top dog!

4013   **Weenie the Dog**   ☐
          CURRENT
COMMENTS: Issued 1996, Birthday 7/20/95, Issue Price $5-$6
This top dog introduced himself with a third generation tag and
now wears a fourth generation tag. He was found with an upside-
down nose! Bongo and Twigs tags have shown up on some of this
Beanie. He was very scarce after January '97 through the "dry"
spring and early summer!
Secondary Market Value: S/S $14-$18
Purchase Date_____ From_____ Price Paid $ _____

Wrinkles™ the Bulldog

This little dog is named Wrinkles
His nose is soft and often crinkles
Likes to climb up on your lap
He's a cheery sort of chap!

4103   **Wrinkles the Bulldog**   ☐
            CURRENT
COMMENTS: Issued 1996, Birthday 5/1/96, Issue Price $5-$6
This Old English Bull dog has shown up with an upside-down nose
and also one ear. Wrinkles comes with a fourth generation tag. A
favorite of many! Ty Co., has a large and medium sized "Winston"
plush dog to accompany this guy!
G-R-E-A-T!
Secondary Market Value: S/S $10-$12
Purchase Date_____ From_____ Price Paid $ _____

Ziggy™ the Zebra

Ziggy likes soccer - he's a referee
That way he watches the games for free
The other Beanies don't think it's fair
But Ziggy the Zebra doesn't care!

4063   **Ziggy the Zebra**   ☐
                CURRENT
COMMENTS: Issued 1995, Birthday 12/24/95, Issue Price $5-$6
Simple tag mistakes such as an "its" instead of "it's" show up on
this striped fellow's poem. Ziggy has been found with the oddity
of one eye being smaller than the other. Tagging problems, such as
no tush tag or misprinted tags, have been found on this striped
wonder. He's an added color plus when looking at the collection!
Secondary Market Value: S/S $10-$12
Purchase Date_____ From_____ Price Paid $ _____

Zip the Cat

Keep Zip by your side all the day through
Zip is good luck, you'll see it's true
When you have something you need to do
Zip will always believe in you!

4004   **Zip the Cat**   1 2 3

CURRENT

COMMENTS: Issued 1994, Birthday 3/28/94, Issue Price $5-$6
Zip zagged through the stores in three different varieties. He was
first larger in size with a triangular shaped muzzle, white underbelly,
and pink ears, nose and whiskers. Eyes were smaller than on the
present cats, paws were body color and he came with a second or
third generation tag. The secondary market price for this Version 1 is
$200-$325. The Version 2 Zip is a rare find. He is smaller and all one
color with the exception of pink on the inside of the ears. His
whiskers are pink, not white, and he has third generation tags and a
black body tag. This Version 2 Zip is sought after at a price of around
$1,000-$1,250. Finally, Version 3 Zip brought white ears, paws and
whiskers. Zip has many various errored tags. Ty's birthday list shows
this cat's birthday as 3/28/93, despite all tags showing 3/28/94.
Secondary Market Value: S/S $10-$12

Purchase Date_____ From_____ Price Paid $ _____

_____

_____

Teenie Beanie Babies™/MC

Snort™/MC

Speedy™/MC

Lizz™/MC

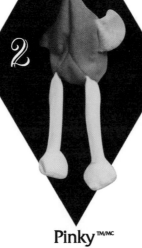
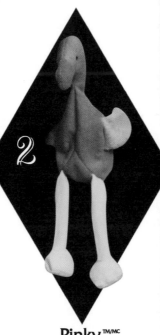

Pinky™/MC

Quacks™/MC

Patti™/MC

Chops™/MC

Seamore™/MC

Chocolate™/MC

Goldie™/MC

Teenie Beanie Babies™/MC

1 Patti™/MC the Platypus ☐

2 Pinky™/MC the Flamingo ☐

3 Chops™/MC the Lamb ☐

4 Chocolate™/MC the Moose ☐

5 Goldie™/MC the Goldfish ☐

6 Speedy™ the Turtle ☐

7 Seamore™/MC the Seal ☐

8 Snort™/MC the Bull ☐

9 Quacks™/MC the Duck ☐

10 Lizz™/MC the Lizard ☐

OUT OF PRODUCTION

COMMENTS: Promo 4/97, Issue Price Free w/McDonald's Happy Meal Also known as McBeanies or TBBs, Teenie Beanies took America by storm in April, during McDonald's five-week Happy Meal promotion that offered two Teenie Beanies per week. The Teenies are listed in the order they were to debut. They came in packages, and are not as collectible unless they are in the bag. (But who wants to display or play with them in a bag?! The package is numbered as per Teenie 1 through 10 as seen above.) Teenie Beanies are smaller than regular-sized Beanie Babies and have embroidered eyes, nose, etc. They also have a single heart swing tag. Demand exceeded the supply of 100 million Teenie Beanies as these sold out at most restaurants VERY quickly, not even lasting the full five weeks! Some restaurants sold them for $1.49 each, gave one with a Happy Meal and limited the purchases. In other areas they had no limits. No doubt, another promotion could be coming our way some day.

It has been **rumored** that future McDonald's Teenie Beanies may be Peace, Rover, Doodle and Bongo. It doesn't matter…"Happy Meal, Please!"

Secondary Market Value: S/S $75-$110 (set of 10)

Purchase Date_____ From_____ Price Paid $ _____

A Rare Bear

Teddy Violet Bear (Rare Bear)

COMMENTS: Issued to Employees and Representatives of Ty. Very Rare Bear! We were lucky to obtain a photograph of him from an anonymous donor. He came with a red ribbon around his neck and no swing tag in his ear.

It would be impossible to accurately set a value on this bear as to our knowledge, none have sold on the secondary market.

Birth dates are not always the same as their debut dates.

 January

Jan. 3, 1993: Spot™
Jan. 6, 1993: Patti™
Jan. 13, 1996: Crunch™
Jan. 15, 1996: Mel™
Jan. 18, 1994: Bones™
Jan. 21, 1996: Nuts™
Jan. 25, 1995: Peanut™
Jan. 26, 1996: Chip™

February

Feb. 1, 1996: Peace™
Feb. 13, 1995: Stinky™
Feb. 13, 1995: Pinky™
Feb. 14, 1994: Valentino™
Feb. 17, 1996: Baldy™
Feb. 20, 1996: Roary™
Feb. 22, 1995: Tank™
Feb. 25, 1994: Happy™
Feb. 27, 1996: Sparky™
Feb. 28, 1995: Flip™

March

Mar. 2, 1995: Coral™
Mar. 6, 1994: Nip™
Mar. 8, 1996: Doodle™
Mar. 14, 1994: Ally™
Mar. 19, 1996: Seaweed™
Mar. 21, 1996: Fleece™
Mar. 28, 1994: Zip™

 April

Apr. 3, 1996: Hoppity™
Apr. 12, 1996: Curly™
Apr. 18, 1995: Ears™
Apr. 19, 1994: Quackers™
Apr. 23, 1993: Squealer™
Apr. 25, 1993: Legs™
Apr. 27, 1993: Chocolate™

May

May 1, 1995: Lucky™
May 1, 1996: Wrinkles™
May 2, 1996: Pugsly™
May 3, 1996: Chops™
May 10, 1994: Daisy™
May 11, 1995: Lizzy™
May 13, 1993: Flash™
May 15, 1995: Tabasco™
May 15, 1995: Snort™
May 19, 1995: Twigs™
May 21, 1994: Mystic™
May 28, 1996: Floppity™
May 30, 1996: Rover™

June

Jun. 1, 1996: Hippity™
Jun. 3, 1996: Freckles™
Jun. 8, 1995: Bucky™
Jun. 8, 1995: Manny™
Jun. 11, 1995: Stripes™

Jun. 15, 1996: Scottie™
Jun. 17, 1996: Gracie™
Jun. 19, 1993: Pinchers™
Jun. 27, 1995: Bessie™

July

Jul. 1, 1996: Pride™
Jul. 1, 1996: Scoop™
Jul. 1, 1996: Maple™
Jul. 2, 1995: Bubbles™
Jul. 4, 1996: Lefty™
Jul. 4, 1996: Righty™
Jul. 8, 1993: Splash™
Jul. 14, 1995: Ringo™
Jul. 15, 1994: Blackie™
Jul. 19, 1995: Grunt™
Jul. 20, 1995: Weenie™

August

Aug. 1, 1995: Garcia™
Aug. 9, 1995: Hoot™
Aug. 13, 1996: Spike™
Aug. 14, 1994: Speedy™
Aug. 17, 1995: Bongo™
Aug. 17, 1995: Nana™
Aug. 23, 1995: Digger™
Aug. 27, 1995: Sting™
Summer 1996: Libearty™
Atlanta, Georgia, USA™

September

Sep. 3, 1995: Inch™
Sep. 3, 1996: Claude™
Sep. 5, 1995: Magic™

September continued...

Sep. 12, 1996: Sly™
Sep. 16, 1995: Kiwi™
Sep. 16, 1995: Derby™
Sep. 18, 1995: Tusk™

October

Oct. 3, 1996: Bernie™
Oct. 9, 1996: Doby™
Oct. 12, 1996: Tuffy™
Oct. 16, 1995: Bumble™
Oct. 17, 1996: Dotty™
Oct. 22, 1996: Snip™
Oct. 30, 1995: Radar™
Oct. 31, 1995: Spooky™

November

Nov. 6, 1996: Pouch™
Nov. 9, 1996: Congo™
Nov. 14, 1993: Cubbie™
Nov. 14, 1993: Brownie™
Nov. 14, 1994: Goldie™
Nov. 21, 1996: Nanook™
Nov. 28, 1995: Teddy Brown™
Nov. 29, 1994: Inky™

December

Dec. 2, 1996: Jolly™
Dec. 8, 1996: Waves™
Dec. 12, 1996: Blizzard™
Dec. 14, 1996: Seamore™
Dec. 16, 1995: Velvet™
Dec. 19, 1995: Waddle™
Dec. 21, 1996: Echo™
Dec. 24, 1995: Ziggy™

Retired

After spending time in stores everywhere, the following Beanie Babies retired.

1996:

Bronty™ the Brontosaurus
Caw™ the Crow
Chilly™ the Polar Bear
Flutter™ the Butterfly
Humphrey™ the Camel
Peking™ the Panda Bear
Rex™ the Tyrannosaurus
Slither™ the Snake
Steg the™ Stegosaurus
Trap the™ Mouse
Teddy™ Cranberry
Teddy™ Jade
Teddy™ Magenta
Teddy™ Teal
Teddy™ Violet
Web™ the Spider

1997

Bubbles™ the Fish
Chops™ the Lamb
Coral™ the Fish
Digger™ the Crab
Flash™ the Dolphin
Garcia™ the Bear
Grunt™ the Razorback
Kiwi™ the Toucan
Lefty™ the Donkey
Libearty™ the Bear
Manny™ the Manatee
Radar™ the Bat
Righty™ the Elephant

Sparky™ the Dalmatian
Splash™ the Orca Whale
Sting™ the Stingray
Tabasco™ the Bull
Tusk™ the Walrus

Replaced but not forgotten, these Beanie Babies are not in production any longer.

Out Of Production

Bongo™ (Version 1)
Brownie™ the bear
Derby™ (Version 1)
Happy™ (Version 1)
Inch™ (Version 1)
Inky™ (Version 1)
Lizzy™ (Version 1)
Lucky™ (Versions 1 & 3)
Magic™ (Version 2)
Mystic™ (Version 2)
Nana™ the monkey
Nip™ (Versions 1 & 2)
Patti ™ (Version 2)
Peanut™ (Version 1)
Pride™ the Bear
Quackers™ (Version 1)
Sly™ (Version 1)
Spot™ (Version 1)
Stripes™ (Versions 1 & 2)
Tank™ (Versions 1 & 2)
Teddy™ Brown (Old Face)
Zip™ (Versions 1 & 2)

Peggy and Dan Gallagher displayed several endangered species at Rosie's Semi-Annual Midwest Collectibles Fest, held in Westmont, IL.

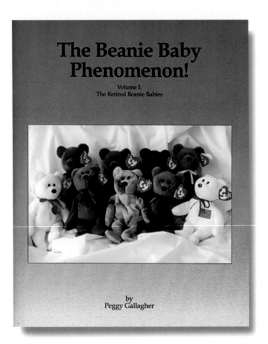

The Beanie Baby Phenomenon!

Volume 1
The Retired Beanie Babies

By: Peggy Gallagher

Peggy and her husband, Dan, have been big contributors
to this guide. Peggy has been collecting Beanie Babies™
almost since day one! Most of the "rare" Beanie Babies™
in this guide are Peggy's! Peggy and Dan are seminar
speakers at our Beanie Fests that are held semi-annually.
Peggy is worth her weight in Beanie Babies™ for sure!

Volume 2 to be
released March 1998!

To Order Call !

1-800-409-8370

Notes

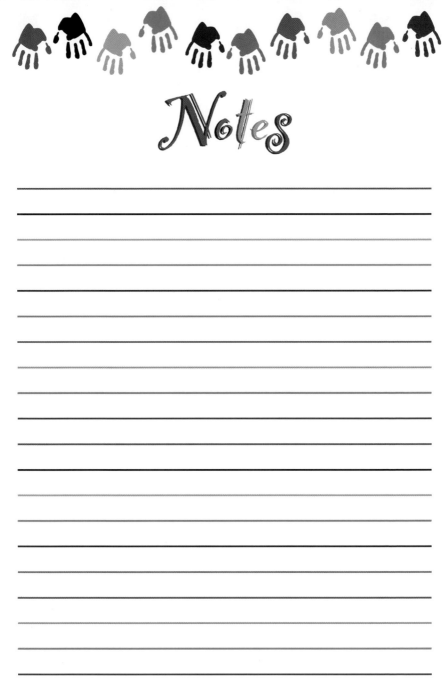

Notes

Notes

Notes

My Personal
Beanie Babies™ Collection

Alligator
☐ Ally™.....................1

Armadillo
☐ Tank™.................102

Bat
☐ Radar™.................76

Bears
☐ Blackie™.................5
☐ Brownie™.............10
☐ Cubbie™.................23
☐ Curly™..................24
☐ Garcia™.................39
☐ Libearty™..............54
☐ Maple™ 59
☐ Peace™.................67
☐ Pride™..................59
☐ Teddy Brown™....103
☐ Teddy Cranberry™104
☐ Teddy Jade™.......105
☐ Teddy Magenta™106
☐ Teddy Teal™.......107
☐ Teddy Violet™.....108
☐ Valentino™..........113

Beaver
☐ Bucky™.................12

Bee
☐ Bumble™..............13

Bulls
☐ Snort™..................89
☐ Snort™(TBB).......122
☐ Tabasco™.............101

Bunnies
☐ Ears™....................31
☐ Floppity™.............36
☐ Hippity™...............44
☐ Hoppity™.............46

Butterfly
☐ Flutter™................37

Camel
☐ Humphrey™.........47

Cats
☐ Chip™...................16
☐ Flip™....................35
☐ Nip™....................64
☐ Snip™...................88
☐ Zip™....................121

Cows
☐ Bessie™..................4
☐ Daisy™..................25

Crabs
☐ Claude™...............19
☐ Digger™................27

Crow
☐ Caw™...................14

Dinosaurs
☐ Bronty™..................9
☐ Rex™.....................77
☐ Steg™....................97

Dogs
☐ Bernie™...................3
☐ Bones™...................7
☐ Doby™...................28
☐ Dotty™...................30

Dogs Continued...
☐ Nanook™...............63
☐ Pugsley™..............74
☐ Rover™..................81
☐ Scottie™................83
☐ Sparky™................90
☐ Spot™...................95
☐ Tuffy™.................110
☐ Weenie™.............118
☐ Wrinkles™...........119

Dolphins
☐ Echo™..................32
☐ Flash™..................33

Donkey
☐ Lefty™..................52

Dragon
☐ Magic™.................57

Ducks
☐ Quackers™............75
☐ Quacks™(TBB)....122

Eagle
☐ Baldy™....................2

Elephant
☐ Peanut™................68
☐ Righty™................78

Fish
☐ Bubbles™..............11
☐ Coral™..................21
☐ Goldie™................40
☐ Goldie™(TBB).....122

TBB = McDonald's Teenie Beanies

Flamingo
☐ Pinky™.................71
☐ Pinky™(TBB).......122
Fox
☐ Sly™.....................87
Frog
☐ Legs™..................53
Ghost
☐ Spooky™.............94
Giraffe
☐ Twigs™...............112
Gorilla
☐ Congo™................20
Hippo
☐ Happy™...............42
Horse
☐ Derby™.................26
Inchworm
☐ Inch™....................48
Kangaroo
☐ Pouch™................72
Koala
☐ Mel™....................60
Ladybug
☐ Lucky™.................56
Lambs
☐ Chops™................18
☐ Chops™(TBB) 122
☐ Fleece™................34
Leopard
☐ Freckles™.............38
Lion
☐ Roary™.................80
Lizards
☐ Lizz™(TBB).........122
☐ Lizzy™..................55
Lobster
☐ Pinchers™............70

Manatee
☐ Manny™...............56
Manta Ray
☐ Sting™..................98
Monkeys
☐ Bongo™...................8
☐ Nana™..................62
Moose
☐ Chocolate™..........17
☐ Chocolate™(TBB)122
Mouse
☐ Trap™.................109
Octopus
☐ Inky™....................49
Otter
☐ Seaweed™............85
Owl
☐ Hoot™..................45
Panda Bear
☐ Peking™................69
Panther
☐ Velvet™..............114
Pelican
☐ Scoop™.................82
Penguin
☐ Waddle™...........115
Pig
☐ Squealer™............96
Platypus
☐ Patti™...................66
☐ Patti™(TBB) 122
Polar Bear
☐ Chilly™.................15
Raccoon
☐ Ringo™.................79
Razorback
☐ Grunt™.................42

Rhino
☐ Spike™..................92
Rooster
☐ Doodle™...............29
Seal
☐ Seamore™............84
☐ Seamore™(TBB) .122
Shark
☐ Crunch™...............22
Skunk
☐ Stinky™.................99
Snake
☐ Slither™................86
Snow Tiger
☐ Blizzard™...............6
Spider
☐ Web™.................117
Squirrel
☐ Nuts™...................65
Swan
☐ Gracie™...............41
Tiger
☐ Stripes™.............100
Toucan
☐ Kiwi™...................51
Turtle
☐ Speedy™..............91
☐ Speedy™(TBB) ...122
Unicorn
☐ Mystic™................61
Walrus
☐ Jolly™...................50
☐ Tusk™.................111
Whales
☐ Splash™................93
☐ Waves™..............116
Zebra
☐ Ziggy™...............120